In The Flow

BRIDGING THE SCIENCE AND PRACTICE OF MINDFULNESS

Deborah Norris Ph.D.

ISBN-13: 9781545188019
ISBN-10: 1545188017
Library of Congress Control Number: 2017905398
CreateSpace Independent Publishing Platform
North Charleston, South Carolina

In The Flow

In the Flow

By Deborah Norris, Ph.D.

Dr. Deborah Norris and her two daughters, Jessie Taylor and Jacqueline Norris, are the Founders and Directors of The Mindfulness Center head-quartered in Bethesda, Maryland. Dr. Norris is also the Director of the Psychobiology of Healing Program in the Department of Psychology at American University, in Washington, D.C., and conducts research at the Veteran's Affairs Medical Center and at the Children's National Health Center in Washington, D.C.

How to Use This Book

THERE ARE MANY STRUGGLES ALONG *the journey of life, such as coping with stress, loss and grief, ill health, relationship problems, job stress, and other modern day issues. This book describes a way to ease and perhaps enlighten the journey. You may recognize the struggle, but may or may not recognize the causes of the struggle. In your search to improve your health, both physical and mental, to find a new partner or better way to live with your current partner, or to maneuver through job-related issues, or simply find a better attitude for coping with the stressors of life, you will find in this book what we are all seeking, a way to get In the Flow.*

As you read this book, note your experience. It is not only the words, but also the effect of the words that you may wish to consider. Words are energy. We convey energy from one person to another with our words. We can affect the way that people feel, with words. With written words, we can convey an experience. Any elementary school English teacher will tell you that good writing involves conveying an experience. Written words can convey this experience across a culture, or across the world. And they can convey this experience across time. As we explore the mechanisms of meditation in this book and the dynamics of the personal experience along the way, let go of your conscious focus on the meaning of the words and become aware of your personal experience of the effect of these words. You may reread the words and shift your focus from the meaning or implications of the words to the experience of the words, and their effect on you.

In all cases, enjoy, and may you find that for which you are looking.

Acknowledgements

I WISH TO EXPRESS MY loving gratitude to my lifelong friend, guru, partner, lover, and husband, Jon Norris, for traveling this journey with me. Ours is an archetypical love.

Jessie and Jacque, my daughters, you are with me day and night as we build and do the work of The Mindfulness Center, a place of healing and joy for ourselves and others. This book is about our work. Thank you for sharing it and continuing to commit your lives to this work. We have found our flow!

Jon, my son, thank you for being my inspiration. It is you who asked me to write this book. It is you who most eagerly holds it by your heart and drinks in its words. It is dedicated to you.

I also wish to thank my many teachers who are the fabric of my life. Thank you first to Evelyn de la Tour. Though your classes were called Modern Dance, what you taught me was to use my body to feel and express. From the sense of tall wheat waving in the breeze and glowing golden in the summer sun, I learned my earliest experiences of shifting energy with my imagination. You taught me the freedom to love and to sense the flowing energies of the world. Thank you Julie and Mary Craighill, who brought me to ballet and continued my lessons in the use of the body, its alignment, and its potential. Thank you Beth Channock. Your awe and delight in my choreography gave me inspiration and a sense of freedom to create. Dr. Tony Riley, you have been a rock in my life.

A very special thank-you to Dr. Rudolph Bauer. As you have for thousands of people, you have changed the path of my life. I have heard you described as a miracle worker. Thank you for teaching me about miracles.

My life and work revolve around the team of people who support me with both their friendship and their shared belief in the mission of bringing mindfulness to all dimensions of life. With love and gratitude, thank you Aurora Hutchinson, Roxanne Lerner, Ada Huang, and the rest of the team at The Mindfulness Center.

Introduction

In the Flow: Bridging the Science and Practice of Mindfulness is a book about how to meditate and how to use meditation as a tool to get back into the flow in life. It provides an evidence-based discussion of how meditation works and why meditation works.

Stress is ubiquitous. The pace of life seems to have accelerated, and people are searching for ways to ease the struggle. As one of my meditation students put it, "I'm looking for a way to live, not just survive." Each time that I ask a new student in my class why they have come to learn to meditate, they usually reply it is to deal with stress or to slow down the speed at which their mind is running. A few students come to meditation to deal with mental or physical health conditions. Fewer admit to relationship problems, but in private this is an underlying issue. Many are struggling at their jobs or are in an awkward phase of career or other life transition.

The truth is that there is a solution to these issues. We have found a resolution for the struggle. *In the Flow* describes the use of meditation to create a beautiful, thriving life—a life of contentment and ease, or perhaps the inspiration to take action for necessary change. It is a discussion of being in the flow, using meditation and other mind–body practices to find the flow. =The underlying current of the book is that meditation processes and outcomes are based in sound science. As a neurobehavioral scientist fluent in the scientific literature and research, I've included interesting and easy–to–understand descriptions of the process and function of meditation. Understanding the mechanisms of action of meditation, the reader is encouraged to further explore the practice and is given images to effectuate their practice.

The more profound effect of the book, however, is that personal experience is the true teacher. The book is written to create an experience, transforming the reader in the process.

The National Center for Complementary and Integrative Health (NCCIH) at the National Institutes of Health (NIH) has followed a grassroots upwelling of interest in mind-body practices. The first phase of their existence was to query whether any of these practices had an effect on mental or physical health or other quality of life. Upon discovering the profound effects of mind-body practices such as meditation, the second phase of inquiry has been to study how it is possible that meditation produces such profound effects in so many dimensions of life and well-being. These "mechanisms of action" have now been well-defined, including the biochemical changes that occur with meditation, the neuroplasticity of specific structures in the brain resulting from different practices, and even recent epigenetic discoveries that meditation can alter our very genes.

As a result of this apparently unexpected discovery of the clear and profound mechanisms by which meditation alters all measurable dimensions of human form and function, the third and current trend in NCCIH's inquiry is to explore just exactly what it is that people are doing when they are so-called "meditating"? If we can practice something that changes us so profoundly, *what exactly is it* that we are doing when sitting on the cushion meditating? What is the practice of meditation? What are the active ingredients? How is it done, and what are the parts of the practice that make a difference? *In the Flow* is a description of the processes and practice of meditation. In reading about the active ingredients of mind-body practices, the reader actually experiences the shift. If swimming against the current is not working, and large numbers of people have a sense of desperation if not outright drowning, *In the Flow* is about a way to change course and to get *In the Flow*.

Table of Contents

PART 1

Finding the Flow

CHAPTER 1
The Flow

MUCH IS SAID THESE DAYS about being "in the moment." We long for the stillness that allows us to let go of the busyness of our lives. We yearn for an easier pace and the opportunities to enjoy the simple things in life. The elusive moment is frustratingly hard to capture. The instant we go to observe the moment, it has already passed. Like the elusive electron circling the atom, in looking for it, scientists can only tell that it has been and may come again, but they cannot actually capture it in any one location in space. Similarly, we demark time in increments by the ticking of a clock, but time is actually in a constant flow.

The word "moment" is derived from the word momentum. Being in the moment is not about capturing any one instant in time. To be in the moment refers to being connected with the momentum of the ever-changing flow in and around us. It is about connecting our consciousness to the flow of the many cycles and rhythms that create the environment of our experience. What we notice when we explore our experience of being in the moment is actually more like a sense of *flow*, a sense of the ever-shifting rhythms around us and within. We come to the practice of meditation to seek stillness and instead we find movement, the cycle of thoughts as they stream through our brains, the constant ebb and flow of our breath, perhaps the pulsing of our hearts, the passing of the day, and other cycles of energy flow generated by the universe around us.

When not in the flow, we may find our thoughts directed toward the future. Concerns about the future can lead to apprehension, anxiety, and stress or compulsive/superstitious behaviors. Alternatively, enthusiasm about the future results in hope or optimism. Another possibility is that our thoughts are directed toward the past. In this case, we may spend time in remorse or regret. Alternatively, the flip side of remorse or regret is a longing for the "Good Old Days."

In the flow, we do not experience these judgmental feelings of the past or of the future. Curiosity about the experience of the ever-moving flow evolves to senses of awe and wonder. Our consciousness fills with a sense of peace as we synchronize with the momentum of the flow in and around us.

Being in the flow allows for the stream of consciousness that may be moving through the brain. Once we recognize this sense of flow within, we can be more accepting of it. Thoughts move. Good ones and bad ones, they move on. The flow may shift from thoughts that we are generating to thoughts that we are receiving, as we open our awareness and let it connect with the greater experience of being. Expanding our awareness allows us to synchronize with the flow.

Once we become aware that thoughts are our interpretation of a stream of energy flowing through our heads, specifically our brains, we may begin to discover ways to regulate this stream of energy flow. As we cultivate mindfulness through the practice of meditation, our consciousness awakens to a sense of clarity and a sense of self. We are able to use this inner sense of being in the flow to connect more harmoniously with the world around us, finding and fulfilling our life's purpose.

CHAPTER 2

The Practice

PEOPLE COME TO THE PRACTICE of meditation along different paths in life. Many people come to meditate as a popular practice to reduce stress, anxiety, or for other health related conditions. Some people turn to meditation to slow down the activity in their brain and to find greater peace of mind. Others try meditation because their doctor, therapist, or friend recommends it. And many people use meditation as a spiritual practice. Consider what brings you to the practice and check in on yourself as you read, and even other times of the day, to discover when things shift for you, as you begin to find that sense of flow.

Meditation is a practice that extends across all cultures of the world and as far back through the ages as human history. As with other practices, such as physical exercise, there are different forms of meditation. What all practices share in common is the use of a single point of mental focus to begin to still the mind. Some people meditate by focusing on a sound such as "om" or a single note. Others chant or meditate on a mantra, such as a word or phrase said over and over again. Other meditation practices focus on an external noise, such as the tone of a chime or singing bowl. A visual focal point may be a candle or a fixed point in a room. Focal points can also be interoceptive, that is, sensations arising from within your body. One such interoceptive practice is to focus on the breath.

In mindfulness meditation, once the mind is stilled, we can let go of our point of focus and be in a curious state of awareness. The practice of using a single point of focus to still the mind and then letting go of that focus and allowing the consciousness to expand into the primordial field of awareness is at least as ancient as recorded history.

CHAPTER 3

Creating Space

SANCTUARY

MEDITATION IS SIMPLY A PRACTICE. Just as going to the gym and working out is a practice, meditation is also a practice that results in long-term changes. As you practice, you will notice a shift, a shift that will permeate your being and your life.

In setting up and establishing your practice, it is good to have a place where you sit regularly to do your practice, a sanctuary. You may wish to create this sanctuary in your home by designing a specific space for your practice. It may be as simple as putting a blanket on a sofa. This blanket can then be transported to another location if you travel. When you put the blanket away, the space can be used for other purposes.

Alternatively, you may wish to create a more elaborate or more permanent space for your practice. You may choose to use candles or dim the lights. You may enjoy background music, or prefer complete silence. Some people like incense or essential oils, while others like fresh air. Bring to your practice any props that you need to make yourself comfortable. Some people prefer sitting upright so that they are less likely to doze off to sleep, and others prefer to recline to allow the body to deeply relax. You may find that on different occasions you prefer different circumstances, so make adjustments as necessary. This is the process of deepening your awareness of your environment and how it affects you and how you can interact with your environment to create a space that supports your practice. Whether your setting is elaborate or minimalist, create your practice space according to your own intention. Many cultures have developed entire fields of study and practice on creating a supportive environment around you, such as the Chinese practices of Feng Shui and the Vedic practices of Vastu. Most cultures have historically recognized the concept of sacred geometry, the potential for our environment to affect our experience. All of these cultural traditions first begin by becoming aware of the environment and making adjustments so that your surroundings are supportive of your sense of well-being.

Environmental Conditioning

As you practice meditation in your sanctuary, the qualities of the space will begin to support your practice. Over time, the sensory stimuli around you will become conditioned to elicit the meditative state. Conditioning to the sensory stimuli in the environment is a psychological phenomenon referred to as environmental conditioning. Environmental conditioning is a well- defined phenomenon in psychology and psychopharmacology. After one or more experiences in a situation or environment, the body begins to anticipate what it expects to occur. The brain begins to make physical adjustments within the body to accommodate the familiar situation. Whether conscious or subconscious, the brain has learned something about the environment and will begin to align us with the environment. If the stimuli in the environment suggest something supportive of our well-being, then the brain will facilitate these supportive actions. For example, when you recognize a safe environment, the body relaxes. If the stimuli in the environment indicate something that will alter your body's normal state of balance and homeostasis, then the brain will begin to create a physical state that is in opposition to this effect, so the sum effect is that the body stays balanced.

Our bodies are designed to be maintained under a certain range of circumstances: a certain range of temperature at which we can function, a certain range of nutrients which we can absorb and turn into fuel, a certain range of hydration, and a certain range of oxygen and other gases which we need to breathe to allow our cells to function properly. All of the functions of our brain and indeed our very genetic makeup are designed to keep us in balance with our environment. When we practice meditation, it is an opportunity for these many systems to come into balance. These systems come into balance both with themselves, and with each other. Our breathing becomes synchronized with our pulse. Our hormones become balanced with our immune system. Our minds become synchronized with our hearts and emotions. Indeed, the entire body has an opportunity to realign itself within, and with the environment around it. We find the opportunity to get into the flow, the rhythm of life.

Meditation is proving to be a non-pharmacological intervention that facilitates the rebalancing of our biochemistry and, consequently, of our lives. Whether a biochemical imbalance is associated with substance use, depression, anxiety, or any other behavioral health concern, the practice of meditation alters our biochemistry in such a way that it alleviates the symptoms and restores us to a more normal state.

When we practice meditation in a specific environment, that environment becomes conditioned to elicit the meditative state. Eventually, the qualities of the environment itself will come to elicit the cascade of biochemical changes that we associate with the state of hedonia (pleasurable state) experienced during meditation. Eventually we need only sit down in this space and we will feel the emotional shift that relieves us from the stresses of the day and allows us to re-center and rebalance.

For example, if you put a blue blanket over your sofa before you sit on it to meditate, and then fold it and put it away until the next time that you practice, you will eventually notice that just the sight of the blue blanket will elicit feelings of relief and equanimity. By thus creating a sanctuary, you can use this sanctuary to support you and your practice. Create a sanctuary that supports your practice, conscious of the role of all of the supporting qualities of the space. Let your attention to the environment around you and your experience of this environment be a part of your practice. In stressful times, your sanctuary or special place for meditation will quickly provide you with relief and a sense of rebalancing. In good times, it will support you in expanding your practice and staying in the flow.

When my husband, Jon, first joined me in meditating, we used to practice in the home of our friend and colleague, Rudy Bauer, Ph.D. Dr. Bauer is the Founder and Director of the Washington Center for Consciousness Studies, and he and his wife Sharon conduct meditation sessions in their home in Washington, D.C. We would gather in large groups in the basement of their townhouse. The basement is a relatively small space and has such a low ceiling that I have to crouch down to walk through it. Yet my husband once remarked about it to friends as a magical space. I retorted that it really was a tiny little basement, but it feels like a magical space. This space has become a conditioned environment for us, a sanctuary supporting our practice.

People often ask me for guidance about how frequently one should meditate. "Do I have to meditate an hour every day?" "Can I meditate once a week?" The truth is that the answer lies within you. As you are mindful of the experience of your practice, you will find a routine that works for you. The practice is self-fulfilling and self-rewarding. Once you start practicing, explore different schedules. I do find that some people like to practice for a full hour every day, and others less frequently. Some people stop and take five-minute meditation breaks several times a day. See what works for you. What works is not so much about how much time you allow yourself the pleasure of meditating, but rather, about whether the practice is enough to make a difference in your life. With all of the findings about the benefits of meditation in many areas of life, is your practice providing you with the benefits that truly make a difference in your life?

Research on the health benefits of beginning a meditation practice shows that significant effects can occur within eight weeks of practice. Most of these studies look at a practice of at least one hour of guided meditation a week, and encourage self-practice during the week. I have seen profound effects even following one session and have a number of students whose self-practice involves one or more five-minute sessions during the day. My research at a national children's hospital has shown that just five minutes of guided meditation can have profound physiological and behavioral effects[1]. Rather than asking for someone else to tell you how to practice, use this as an opportunity to begin self-exploration. The truth is that what works for you at one time may later evolve. The point of the practice is to be able to learn what you need and when, and to be responsive to your needs.

Changes in the brain and, correspondingly, in one's quality of life and health can occur relatively quickly with a meditation practice. Regardless of the type of meditation practice, my research and others' have found significant effects after only eight weeks of practice, and often even shorter terms of practice are producing significant results as well. I repeatedly have students reporting that they have been struggling with physical pain or emotional trauma for years, yet after a single session with me, their pain is completely gone, or they have learned to control their anxiety, panic, or other emotional distress. It may take up to eight weeks to see significant growth in certain brain areas, but in a single session, students can discover how to access that brain region responsible for the healing that we are seeking. Once we have experienced the power of relief from our physical or emotional distress, we are typically drawn back to the practice that affords the relief.

Meditation, as with any practice, creates changes in your brain/physiology and behavior. If you work out at the gym by lifting weights with your arms, your arm muscles will grow but not necessarily your legs or abs. If you work out all of your muscles, you will become strong, not only at the gym but everywhere you go. You will *be* strong. What you practice is what you get. If you practice cultivating ease, you will find that you live life with ease. If you practice cultivating compassion, you will become compassionate. If you practice experiencing joy, you will become joyful. If you practice cultivating conscious awareness, you will become more consciously aware.

Research on these different practices shows that what you practice is what you get. Exercising one part of the brain causes growth in that specific region of the brain, just as the effects of strength training corresponds to the specific muscles that you exercise. When you exercise your biceps, you see growth in the bicep muscle. If you exercise the prefrontal cortex, you will see growth and improved function in the prefrontal cortex.

So choose what you practice with intention. Let a sense of the flow guide you to your practice and through your practice. We are often aware of what we don't want. Indeed, most of my clients come into my office and tell me what they don't want. Practice identifying what you *do* want. Begin to notice what it feels like to have what you want. The next step will be realizing that you have what you want. At the end of meditation practice, I often hear my students say, "I feel like I am who I want to be, and I want to be who I am." Create your own practice. It will serve you best.

CHAPTER 4

Health Effects of Meditation

THE NATIONAL INSTITUTES OF HEALTH (NIH), the largest biomedical research agency in the world, has gradually responded to an upwelling of grassroots interest in mind- body practices, opening the Office of Alternative Medicine in 1991. As the name and the reputation of this office has evolved, becoming the National Center for Complementary and Alternative Medicine in 1998, and the National Center for Complementary and Integrative Health in 2014, so has their research focus. Initial research focused on whether or not there were any clinical health benefits from complementary and alternative medical approaches. The results have been profound, showing effects in all areas of mental and physical health resulting from a broad and diverse number of mind and body practices. Spiritual practices such as prayer are also explored through clinical research trials funded by the NIH. Mindfulness practices have emerged as profoundly effective in treating many diseases. While interest in rigorously defining the benefits of mind- body practices such as meditation through controlled clinical trials still remains today, the focus of their research has expanded.

As the evidence-basis began accumulating for the health benefits of meditation, the focus of research funding and scientific inquiry began to shift. A new funding priority emerged, to define the mechanisms of action by which meditation could have such profound effects. The question became, "If meditation can improve one's health so significantly, *how is it doing this?*" These "mechanisms of action" have now been well defined. A new body of literature delineates the incredible plasticity of the human form, and the practice of meditation as a foundation underlying the capacity for both physical and behavioral change. Meditation has been shown to affect multiple systems of our bodies, including changes in the biochemistry of neurotransmitters, hormones, and immunochemicals; modulation of the neuroplasticity of specific structures in the brain resulting from different practices; and even recent discoveries in the simultaneously emerging field of epigenetics, showing that meditation can alter our very genes and those of our offspring for generations to come.

As a result of these apparently unexpected discoveries of the clear and profound mechanisms by which meditation alters all measurable dimensions of human form and function, a third trend in research priorities at NIH is gradually emerging. A new trend is exploring just exactly what it is that people are doing when they are so-called "meditating." If we can practice something that changes us so profoundly, *what exactly is it that people are doing*? What is the practice of meditation? As you sit on a cushion with your eyes closed, fervently trying to clear your mind and *become a meditator*, what is it that you should be doing? What are the active ingredients? How is it done, and what are the parts of the practice that make a difference? With so many different types of meditation, and even different teachers of the same type of practice guiding differently, how do we know what to practice and how to do it? In the chapters to come, I will describe in detail the elements of the practice that have the most profound health benefits and that lead to the most significant health benefits. As I reveal the active ingredients of meditation, I will also share with you the science that explains how and why these essential elements of the practice work, enabling you to bridge the science and the practice of mindfulness.

DOES IT WORK? CLINICAL EFFECTS

In recent years, researchers have been exploring the clinical benefits of mindfulness practices for treatment of just about every mental and physical health condition known to humankind. One of the earliest clinical findings on the benefits of mindfulness meditation showed that meditation is an effective treatment for disorders of the skin, such as psoriasis.[2] This research opened the door to our awareness that the mind can heal the body. Since then, the practice of meditation has been found to affect health outcomes for most every disease defined by medical science. Research shows that practicing meditation can reduce the incidence of heart disease, including major adverse cardiac events, affecting every risk factor that has been identified to lead to heart disease.[3] Mindfulness has proven to be a useful tool in relieving symptoms of pain for those suffering with arthritis and other forms of chronic pain, including fibromyalgia, low- back pain, lupus, irritable bowel syndrome, Crohn's disease, and more. The medical standard of care for treatment of chronic pain now involves the use of meditation, and not medication, as the first step in treatment, according to the NIH, the Centers for Disease Control and Prevention, and other major hospital systems across the country.

Numerous studies indicate that practicing meditation improves the health status of patients with diabetes.[4] Researchers are now exploring the multiple clinical benefits of mindfulness as an integrative practice in the treatment of cancer, including quality of life and rates of survival. Meditation is also being explored as an intervention for the treatment of acute conditions, such as colds and flu, which have been found to resolve more quickly in people who meditate. Research on the health outcomes of using mindfulness practices as a part of the treatment regimen for people with a diagnosed medical condition will continue to show positive, if not amazing, results as long as we wish to make it a funding priority. In all of this research, I have yet to see results reporting any adverse side effects of the practice of meditation, beyond increased awareness of the healing processes, such as release of past emotional traumas and the pain of wounds. The evidence for the powerful potential of the mind to heal the body through the practice of mindfulness was profound enough to prompt the question: "How could this be?" The next phase of research began the determination of the mechanisms of action of mindfulness—exploring what physiological changes occur during mindfulness practices that are responsible for the benefits we are seeing in the health status of patients who practice.

"What If My Problem Is Biochemical?"

Our bodies are a delicate balance of thousands of different biochemicals that play an important role in keeping us functional in often varying circumstances. One of the important characteristics of these biochemicals is that they are designed to be adaptive to changing environments. As the environment changes, our hormones change; as our mood changes, our neurochemistry is altered. When we eat or get thirsty, all of the varying states of our experience are actually reflected by the activity of the biochemicals in our bodies. Asleep, awake, busy, relaxed, thinking hard or daydreaming, all are associated with changes in our biochemistry. One might even say that the state we are experiencing *is* the state of our biochemistry at any given moment. This system of chemicals is primed and ready to respond to input from the environment in order to shift our state to deal with a wide range of external influences.

There is a misunderstanding that if we have a biochemical imbalance it must be treated with chemicals in order to be corrected. It is true that pharmaceuticals/drugs do act on the same receptor mechanisms as our own system. And we can modulate our systems through the use of exogenous drugs. But it is because there is already a chemically driven system in place in the body that the drugs are able to work.

Just as computer viruses are able to take over an operating system and use the preexisting system for their own purposes, the virus can only function because there is already a system in place. The computer system was built for a different purpose, but the virus is able to change the way that the system functions. Furthermore, if we remove the virus, the operating system is often able to return to its original programming function.

You may wonder, but what if the original operating system is not giving me the outcome that I want? Most outcomes are based on an *"If this, then that"* relationship. *If this* is going on, *then that* must happen. What we are neglecting in the management of chronic diseases in our current system is to look at the original *if this* circumstances. For example, *if* you work in a highly stressful environment, *then* you are more likely to suffer from chronic pain. This programming is not a cry for medication with drugs, but rather a message from the body to meditate and do yoga to relieve stress, sleep better, and feel better.

If someone has recently lost a loved one and is grieving the loss, this is not a biochemical imbalance demanding treatment with drugs. This is a natural response to loss, which will improve, and can improve more quickly for those who learn to meditate and self- regulate their emotions.

The original operating system of our bodies has been ingeniously programmed to adapt to changes in our environment. By learning to meditate, we learn to self-regulate this internal environment. In truth, this self-regulation involves letting the powerful force of our consciousness take control; this same consciousness that regulates the healing of scrapes, cuts, bruises, and broken bones is empowered to heal us of the myriad conditions of human suffering.

The adaptive nature of our biochemical system causes it to react to the presence of drugs, typically in the opposite direction of what we want. If we administer opiates or other narcotics to reduce pain, over time our system adapts by shutting down our own endogenous pain relieving mechanism (known in part as the endorphins). Our system learns to recognize the onset of the drug effect, or the environmental stimuli that predict the onset of the drug effect, and in the presence of these stimuli, to create the opposite effect of the drugs. We become dependent upon the use of drugs to keep us from experiencing pain.

The goal of our brain is to maintain our systems in a balance with our environment. The good news is that, once again due to the adaptive and flexible nature of this system, if we stop taking the drugs, the body learns and gradually reinstates its own endogenous mechanisms for relieving pain. Mindfulness meditation can facilitate this rebalancing of our biochemistry during withdrawal; and helps us to maintain optimal functioning following recovery of homeostasis.

These same adaptive mechanisms exist for all of the biochemicals in our body associated with the various mood states that we can experience. If we take drugs to make us feel happy, we are even less able to find our own resources for being happy and we become dependent upon medication to relieve despair. If we drink coffee to boost our energy, we become dependent upon coffee to keep us going. If we use alcohol to sedate our frazzled nerves, we become dependent upon alcohol to relieve us of stress and anxiety. All of these drugs, including alcohol, caffeine, and many other mood altering chemicals, are able to have an effect on us because we already have a system in place to regulate these moods. The drugs are simply acting on this preexisting system.

When we experience a mood, such as anxiety or depression, the system is not malfunctioning. The system is being activated by something that is causing us to be uncomfortable. If the mood altering drugs are able to have an effect, then there are naturally occurring endogenous chemicals that could be activated to do the same thing. A more effective and long-lasting solution than taking drugs is to learn techniques for modulating one's own biochemistry.

We modulate our own biochemistry in many ways. Each time you are hungry and you eat and feel full you have done something to change the chemistry of your body. Putting food in your body results in a change in the way you feel. Every time you get tired and lie down to sleep and awaken rested you have taken an action that changes your chemistry and consequently the way you feel. Have you ever exercised and paused to notice how you feel afterward? Or perhaps you've turned on music and noticed that it can change your mood? You may notice that being around certain people or in certain environments changes the way that you feel. This is because these environmental stimuli affect your biochemistry. By changing the environment or the people around you, you have found a way to alter your own biochemistry. The actions and activities of your own behavior have mood-altering effects of their own. You can learn to use these behavioral tools to affect your mental and emotional health. Research on all of these lifestyle factors has proven that lifestyle factors have powerful effects on your biochemistry and, consequently, your mood and well-being.

I identify six primary lifestyle factors: Stress management/meditation, sufficient sleep, adequate hydration, adequate exercise, good nutrition, and social interaction/a sense of community. In this book, I focus on meditation as a practice for stress management.

Meditation is the practice of sitting in quiet reflection and literally fine-tuning your biochemistry and your corresponding mood. Though you may or may not interpret it that way, you will eventually notice the effects of meditation on how you feel. Once you are conscious of what you are doing in your practice, you can get right to the heart of it and focus on creating a chemical/physical state that pleases you. As with any practice, it may take some time to master, but the more you practice, the more masterful you will become.

Neurofeedback practices have shown us that we can learn to self-modulate our nervous system.[5] Real-time functional magnetic--resonance imaging (fMRI) permits simultaneous measurement and observation of brain activity during an ongoing task. Research using real-time fMRI measures shows us that we can acquire volitional control of localized brain activity. That is, with practice, we can intend to activate a specific part of the brain. Not only can we learn to control activity in a specific region of the brain, but also this self-regulation activity leads to specific changes in our emotions and behavior. That is, we can intend to change the way that we think and behave. This self-awareness that we have using fMRI leads to the capacity for self-control and self-regulation. Mindfulness practices, particularly those focused on interoceptive self-awareness, are another way of learning to self- modulate. Mindful awareness of the flowing sensations of your feelings reveals the subtle mechanism by which we acquire volitional control of the brain's activity, and the corresponding emotions and behaviors.

The physical effects of meditation on our bodies have been explored in great detail. We now know that meditation has profound effects on every system of the body, including the biochemicals of our nervous, immune, and endocrine systems. For example, meditation has been shown to increase levels of endorphins, the body's own pain relieving chemicals. Known as the endogenous opiates, endorphins regulate feelings of pleasure and pain, as well as digestion.

Meditation has also been shown to increase levels of the neurotransmitter, serotonin. Serotonin is believed to regulate our mood. It is this reasoning behind the development of serotonin- selective reuptake inhibitors such as Prozac, Paxil, Celexa, Zoloft, and many other drugs designed to modulate serotonin levels and possibly relieve people from depression. Practicing meditation can have the same effects on relieving depression as medication, with researchers suggesting that meditation "offers protection against relapse/recurrence (of depression) on a par with that of maintenance antidepressant pharmacotherapy."[6]

Serotonin also plays a critical role in regulating our immune system. Several studies have shown that serotonin itself causes apoptosis (cell-death) of certain types of cancer cells. Specifically, researchers found that serotonin efficiently and markedly suppresses the DNA of Burkett's Lymphoma (BL) cells.[7] Another study suggested that serotonin can "drive rapid and extensive apoptosis in biopsy-like BL cells."[8] Since meditation effectively increases circulating levels of serotonin in the body, the results of these studies suggest that serotonin's role as both neurotransmitter and immunomodulator may prove to be part of the mechanisms by which meditation improves mood, quality of sleep, feelings of well-being, and rates of survival in individuals with cancer. Further research is needed to determine the role of meditation in cancer prevention and treatment and to define the specific mindfulness practices with the greatest impact on well-being.

Diabetes is another condition that is improved by the practice of meditation. Research has shown that practicing meditation improves glycemic control and insulin function and relieves oxidative damage to the beta cells of the pancreas, which are responsible for production of insulin. By regulating blood sugar levels, decreasing insulin resistance, and improving pancreatic beta cell function, meditation may play an important role in the prevention and treatment of both Type I and Type II diabetes.[9] [10]

Meditation also improves mental health conditions such as general psychological distress, anxiety, and post-traumatic stress disorder (PTSD). Practicing meditation to reduce stress lowers production of cortisol, prevents adrenal fatigue, and normalizes a lengthy cascade of hormonal functions that are disrupted by the stress response.

Many other biochemicals are also affected by the self-modulating practice of meditation. Oxytocin, the famous "love hormone," so-called because it is secreted when nursing a baby and at times of orgasm, is also released during meditation. Meditation has been shown to regulate levels of melatonin, which induces sleep. Even growth hormone, which plays a role in growth and healing, is affected by the practice of meditation. Meditation has also been found to regulate inflammatory responses in the nervous system and associated sensations of pain throughout the body.[11]

It seems that with the right type of self-awareness practice, we can learn to self-regulate just about every operating system in our bodies. Until the recent explosion of interest and research on the mechanisms of action of mindfulness practices, we have tinkered with the biochemistry of our body, prodding it and exploring it, like playing a crap shoot, with drugs. Having been involved in drug development for the National Institute of Drug Abuse, I am well aware of the uncertainty of the effects of drugs on any one individual. Many people cannot tolerate certain medications that others can. And some drugs have side effects as serious as or potentially worse than the effects for which they are prescribed. Lists of adverse side effects of drugs are lengthy. With mindfulness practices, we have discovered the human being behind the curtain who is actually pulling all of the strings in this mystery we call life. The mindfulness practices of expanding the consciousness give us access to regulate the biochemistry of our own bodies. The Great Oz, the "man behind the curtain," is you and your awareness of self!

By cultivating your meditation practice regularly in a specific environment, characteristics of the environment will become conditioned to elicit this biochemical shift that occurs within your brain and the rest of your body. With practice, you will begin to notice the cascading shift in your biochemistry and correspondingly the feelings and moods that these biochemicals regulate. You will find a way to get in the flow. By learning to titrate your own emotions through the practice of meditation, you can more smoothly

> The important outcome of all of this research on brain mechanisms of meditation is that different meditation practices affect the growth and potential of different brain parts.

manage the ups and downs of life. You will know a way to get back into the flow. Self-prescribing and self-administration of meditation (not medication) will keep you in the flow.

Neuroplasticity: What You Practice Is What You Get

Research on the effects of meditation on the brain has taken our understanding of the infinite potential to create the life of our own choosing to a whole new level. Since the discovery of neuroplasticity, the ability for new neurons to form in the brain, we have learned that our brains and, correspondingly, our behaviors could change. We learned that if the brain was damaged, it could regenerate new cells in the damaged area. Furthermore, function could also be recovered and restored following some types of brain injury.

Early research on the effects of meditation on the brain was eager to identify brain sites responsible for the effects of meditation. Changes in brain function during meditation have been documented using a variety of imaging procedures, including electroencephalography (EEG), single photon emission computed tomography (PET), and fMRI. Reports are abundant defining the parts of the brain affected by meditation.[12] Some researchers report definitively that meditation increases grey matter in the left hippocampus, the anterior cingulate cortex, the temporo- parietal junction, the cerebellum, and the amygdala. Others, however, report effects in the thalamus, insula, or left parietal prefrontal cortex or nucleus accumbens. Some have reported effects in the hippocampus, while still others claim effects in the hypothalamus. Early researchers suggested that when they found an effect in a particular area of the brain, this brain part had to be responsible for all of meditation's amazing outcomes. Scientists are gradually becoming aware that other scientists are finding effects in different areas of the brain. One scientist has even gone so far as to suggest that, "Results (of brain studies) differ somewhat, possibly owing to the use of different forms of meditation."[13] Given the extremely varied effects of meditation on the brain, it is clear that not all forms of meditation produce the same effects on our brains or behavior. The important outcome of all of this research on brain mechanisms of meditation is that different meditation practices affect the growth and potential of different brain parts. Depending upon what we practice, we cultivate different abilities. If we focus on sensations of loving compassion, as in Vipassana meditation, we cultivate growth of neurons in the frontal brain and thalamus, which regulate positive emotions and sensory processes. If we focus on repeating the words of a mantra, as in transcendental meditation, we see growth in the left parietal lobe of the frontal cortex, responsible for processing words. If we practice focusing on a state of ecstatic joy, we see development of the reward centers of the brain, such as the nucleus accumbens, which regulates feelings of pleasure. When we spend time focusing intensively on the sensate experiences of our body, as in yoga nidra, we see activation of the parts of our brain known to regulate interoceptive awareness, such as the anterior cingulate cortex. What you practice is what you get. The lesson is that you should choose a focal point for your practice that supports the type of growth that you want to experience.

If you were to go to the gym and exercise only one set of muscles, you would only see growth in the muscle in that area of the body. For example, if you focus your exercise on your right bicep, you will see growth in your right bicep, but you will not expect to see growth on your left bicep. When you exercise your brain by sitting in one type of meditation practice, you will have growth in the specific brain area that regulates that behavior. Just as with physical exercises, mental exercises deliver exactly what you practice, in the way that you practice it. So practice the experience that you want to cultivate.

There are a number of ways in which you can practice. For example, some people keep a Gratitude Journal, making daily notations about things for which they feel grateful. By practicing the experience of gratitude, people find that they feel grateful more often. In mindfulness meditation we focus not only on thoughts about the emotion, but also the physical feelings in the body that we associate with the emotion, such as sensations in the belly, the heart, the shoulders, or the face.

> **The lesson is that you should choose a focal point for your practice that supports the type of growth that *you want to experience.***

As you continue to cultivate your practice, you will find that mindfulness will permeate more and more of your life. Again, just as one goes to the gym to strengthen their muscles and build endurance, one finds that they still have use of these muscles and endurance even outside of the gym. You become strong. You may have use for your strength when working around the house or in the yard, and as a result of your practice at the gym, you have the strength to use it any time that you like. Similarly, with your meditation practice, you may find yourself outside of your practice, drawing upon your strength in mindfulness and simply being mindful.

Depending upon your mental practice and the specific focus of your meditation, you can change your brain and, correspondingly, your life as you choose. The brain not only regulates and informs one's quality of life, but also it *is* the experience of life. Research on meditation and other mind-body practices is finding that we can create the physical and emotional experience of our own choosing. The limits of this experience have not yet been defined.

Meditation is foundational in behavioral change. It is the practice of cultivating greater ease, peace, compassion, love, joy, bliss, abundance, simplicity, whatever you choose to have in your life, whatever allows you to find the flow.

The power of the placebo effect has been unlocked from its derogatory reputation as a nuisance factor. If the placebo effect can be recognized as the power of belief to affect the outcome of your health, then mindfulness practices can be recognized as the tool for discovering a belief system that works for you. Given research findings on the neuroplasticity of the brain and the corresponding ability to use mindfulness practices to tap into this plasticity and regulate our own behavior and emotions, we are now free to learn, and practice, to create our own beliefs. We can free ourselves from the burdens of fear, despair, and hopelessness and tap into the power of the placebo effect—the power of what we believe. Practicing meditation gives us the power to use our own minds to create the life of our own choosing. In this way, meditation allows us to find and fulfill our life's purpose, and to be *in the flow*.

ELECTROPHYSIOLOGY OF MEDITATION

Another way of studying the functional activities of the brain and the brain's relation to behavior are through the use of EEG. Using EEG we can detect different brain states associated with different wavelengths of electrical energy emanating from our brains. Four primary brain states are identified as beta, alpha, theta, and delta, corresponding with decreasing levels of brain activity.

The highest frequency brain waves are beta waves. Beta waves (at a frequency of brain activity between 12.5 and 30 Hz) are associated with the conscious and awake state, such as when a person is working or carrying on a conversation. Planning and other goal-oriented tasks are detected by different amplitudes of beta waves. Low amplitude beta waves are associated with concentration; decision making; and active, busy, or anxious thinking.

Alpha brain waves are lower frequency (7.5-12.5 Hz) and characteristic of a more relaxed state, like resting with the eyes closed. Even lower frequency theta brain waves (4-7 Hz) tend to appear during drowsy or sleepy states, during REM sleep, and briefly during the transition from sleep to waking. Delta waves, the lowest frequency of brain activity (0.1-4 Hz), are found during deep, slow-wave, non-dreaming sleep.

Research on the effects of meditation on the electrical activity of the brain again appears to be dependent upon the type of meditation that the researchers have been studying. Some studies have reported meditation inducing alpha waves.[14] Others claim that meditation results in theta waves.[15] And yet others find that their practitioners generate delta waves during their practice.[16] Different practices are resulting in different brain waves. Again we find, what you practice is what you get. Different brain states are associated with different healing phenomena. As researchers begin to elucidate the factors associated with the specific brain wave states, practitioners can begin to focus their practice on the types of effects most beneficial to healing themselves, and to their own well-being. We will find that different practices are better for some people than others. Each of us must travel our own journey. Again, we find that we can choose the practice that works best for us. The best guide is to use mindfulness practices to be empowered to explore what is working best for you. In being open-minded and aware, we can fine-tune our practice to give us optimally just what we are looking for in life.

GENETIC EFFECTS OF MEDITATION

Perhaps the most impressive of all of the findings on the mechanisms of action of meditation on the systems of the body is the potential for meditation to alter our genes. Coinciding with recent advances and interest in epigenetics, researchers have been exploring the effects of mindfulness practices on genes, gene expression, and the bodily functions regulated by these genes.[17] [18] Understanding the potential implications of this research requires a quick updating of our knowledge of genetic processes.

Knowing that our entire physical structure and behavioral function are preprogrammed by our genes, geneticists have long been interested in finding a direct relation between the layout of genes on chromosomes and their outcome. The study of this relationship between gene and structure/function is referred to as genetic mapping. The very first gene map was created by Dr. Alfred Sturtevant in 1913 for the *Drosophila* fly.[19] In 1977, Frederick Sanger developed techniques for determining the DNA sequence on genes, for which he received a Nobel Prize in 1980.[20] These DNA sequencing techniques were soon automated and scientists were contemplating the idea of analyzing the entire human genome.

In 1974, I received a National Science Foundation Award to conduct research on behavioral genomics, working with Dr. Ruth Pertel at the NIH, National Institute of Allergies and Infectious Diseases. At that time, leading up to the birth of the Human Genome Project, we were mapping genes for physical and behavioral traits in *c. elegans*, a nematode particularly well-suited to genetic manipulation. *C. elegans* is about as primitive an organism that exists, yet it shares many of the essential biological characteristics of human biology. The worm is conceived as a single cell that undergoes an intricate process of development, starting with embryonic cleavage, proceeding through morphogenesis and maturation. It has a nervous system, including a rudimentary brain. It exhibits behavior and is capable of learning. It produces sperm and eggs; mates and reproduces; and eventually ages, loses vigor, and finally dies.

To map which genes regulate which features in this simple creature, we induced mutations using a known mutagen, ethyl methanesulfonate, and named the six types of mutants "Dumpy," "Uncoordinated," and left and right "Twirlers" and "Rollers." I was lucky enough to be doing this research at an NIH laboratory at a time when significant developments in electron- microscopy made these rare machines commercially available. We were one of the first labs in the country to receive one and to use it to explore the relation between altered genes and altered structure and be-havior. Using an electron microscope, I was the first person to photograph a nematode with a tumor. Dr. Pertel proudly sent this photograph to the Smithsonian Institution for its collection of what I assumed to be a rather bizarre collection of artifacts.

In 1988, Congress formalized the Human Genome Project by creat-ing an agreement between the NIH and the Department of Energy (DOE was at that time concerned about the effects of radiation on *human* muta-tions) to sequence and map all of the genes of humans. The project was officially launched in 1990, and since that time the majority of the human genome has been sequenced, giving us the ability to read nature's complete genetic blueprint for building a human being.[21] Some of the interesting facts revealed from this project are the relatively small number of human genes (about 30,000) and the relative similarity of the human genome to that of other animals such as *c. elegans.*

It is often assumed that if something is *genetic*, then it is a mandatory, unavoidable trait of the organism. A common misunderstanding is that a trait or characteristic is either caused by our genes, or caused by our environment. Indeed, most traits are both. A more accurate perspective is that our genes provide a predisposition for a trait. Often referred to as the blueprint for life, our genes give us the *potential* to develop or to function in a certain way. Just as a blueprint provides a specific layout for a building, the actual materials used in the building will make a significant difference in the final appearance and functions of the building. In this same way, the environment works on our genetic disposition to influence our appear-ance and function. Many genes do not exert their influence unless they are activated by specific environmental influences. Some environmental stimuli turn on genes, and others may turn genes off. It is not until a gene is *expressed* (turned on) that its potential is activated and its disposition becomes apparent, and the instructions that are encoded within the gene are carried out.

When a gene is turned on, it tells other cells what to do. Gene expression is the process by which genetic instructions are used to synthesize gene products that organisms need to survive. These products are usually proteins such as enzymes, hormones, and receptors, which perform essential functions. Not all genes or their products are needed at all times. For example, some gene products are used to terminate the life of a cell and are therefore only expressed at the end of a cell's life. Other genes activate cellular metabolism and improve cellular respiration. Others encode for inflammation, and yet others block inflammation from occurring. Some genes activate while others suppress tumor growth and the development of cancer. Others activate regeneration of healthy new cell growth.

Normal healthy function requires the capability of all of our genes to operate when they are called upon. One of the ways in which we define the aging process is when genes begin to fail to operate as they are programmed. A specific indicator of aging is when chromosomes begin to deteriorate and gene regulation is impaired. As chromosomes deteriorate, the ends of the DNA strands, referred to as telomeres, literally break off, resulting in shorter and functionally impaired chromosomes. When telomeres are not replaced on the ends of chromosomes and these strands of DNA become shorter, cellular repair and other key functions of the systems of our body start to fail. The blueprint for the functions of life starts to fade. We call this ill-health or disease. All chronic diseases such as heart disease, diabetes, and cancer are associated with shorter strands of DNA. It sounds bad, but there is actually good news.

In healthy cells, chromosomal length and function is maintained by an enzyme referred to as telomerase. Telomerase literally puts the telomeres back on the ends of the chromosomes. As telomerase levels decline, chromosomes start to fall apart and become shorter. Low levels of telomerase are associated with cardiovascular disease, obesity, high levels of stress and stress hormones, inflammation, and anemia. Fortunately, if and when telomerase levels increase, shortened chromosomes can be repaired, and normal function can be reinstated. There is hope. The million-dollar question then is, what can be done to increase levels of telomerase?

One of the more profound discoveries of the effects of meditation on genes is that meditation increases telomerase levels. Dr. Elizabeth Blackburn, who won the Nobel Prize for her discovery of telomerase, and her colleagues have explored the effects of meditation on telomerase activity. Their results found that meditation has significant effects, activating a 43 percent increase in telomerase levels in those who meditated for just eight weeks.[22] This study and others have shown that telomerase activity clearly increases more dramatically with meditation than from any telomerase supplement or drug ever sold. Meditation is the most effective treatment that has ever been found to increase telomerase enzyme activity. Further research will likely continue to explore the logical assumption that by restoring telomerase levels, to some extent mindfulness meditation actually reverses the aging process.

Once again, we may ask, how can this be? How can meditation relieve the processes of aging associated with telomerase decline? One hypothesis is that psychological distress may actually cause telomerase decline, and that mindfulness practices relieve the distress so that telomerase levels can get back to normal.

Clearly, stress is not only uncomfortable but also debilitating to our health. Stressful situations, such as the perception of a threat or danger, activate systems in the body that are crucial to our short-term survival. Systems that are in place to support our long-term survival, such as digestion, reproductive hormone cycles, growth and repair mechanisms, wound healing, bone and muscle repair, are put on hold, so that all of our energy resources can be used for immediate survival. If we don't make it through the moment, all of the long-term survival systems won't be of much use; so why not put all of the resources that we have into getting us out of danger, even if it means we are not digesting, building bones, or producing reproductive hormones for the moment. When we are (or at least feel) safe, then these long-term survival systems can come back into play.

There is even some evidence suggesting that occasionally challenging our ability to move between short-term survival mode and long-term survival mode enhances both. Like heart-rate variability, which is the ability of our heart rate to go up when we are physically challenged and for it to go back down when we rest, the ability for all of our body systems to respond to challenge and then restore resting homeostasis when relieved is an indicator of overall vigor and longevity. It is a sort of cross- training for multiple body systems.

Meditation is a way to reestablish homeostasis of all body systems after and even while dealing with challenge or threat. As a society, we are good at taking on stress and challenge. We seem to take on more and more and have forgotten to take the time to rebalance, get back to resting state, and let our telomerase levels rebound. We are out of practice in being able to both take on challenges, and let go. In this way, the mindfulness practices of letting go make more sense in their health promoting appeal. I once sat through a meditation led by my student who recited over and over, "Let go. Let go. Let go." I get it. Drop the ball. Let everything unravel. Take the weight of the world off of your shoulders. Catch your breath. However you want to say it, taking time out of your day to meditate on letting go of accumulating stress is a key to present moment health and longevity.

Many physical and psychological factors have been associated with stress. A few of these have also been associated with telomerase activity. The ability to reframe stressful situations from threat to challenge has been seen as an outcome of meditation and a factor influencing telomeres/ aging. People who meditate have both a better perspective on stress and higher telomerase levels. Meditation can also alter the degree to which one perceives that they have control over life.[23] Perceived level of control has also been associated with telomerase activity.[24]

Another psychological phenomenon that mediates the effects of mindfulness and stress on telomerase activity is a sense of purpose in life. Studies measuring the extent to which people feel a sense of "Purpose in Life" showed that people who meditate have a greater sense of purpose. Furthermore, having a sense of purpose directly affected perceived control, negative emotionality, and telomerase activity.[25]

People who have a greater sense of purpose are also healthier in other regards. They have higher levels of self-esteem, are less depressed, and report overall better well-being. Using mindfulness to find and fulfill your life's purpose not only creates a more meaningful and enjoyable life, but it may well affect your genes and extend the length of your life. Live long and prosper by using mindfulness to get in the flow, find your passion, and fulfill your life's purpose!

Meditation, Genes, and Cancer

Exciting results on the role of mindfulness in telomerase activity were initially tempered by the consideration that not only might meditation and other mind-body practices increase telomerase function and the viability of chromosomes in healthy cells, but it might also increase the viability of genes regulating cancer cell growth. There was concern that increasing telomerase levels through healthy lifestyle choices such as meditation would increase telomerase levels in cancer cells. While scientists have yet to explore the details of the effect of meditation on telomerase levels in healthy cells versus cancer cells, a study on the effects of acupuncture may suggest the outcome of such a study. Researchers from the Heart Disease Research Foundation in New York found that acupuncture differentially affects telomerase levels in healthy cells and cancer cells. People with lung cancer who received acupuncture showed significant decreases in telomeres of the cancer cells, while the telomere length of healthy cells increased.[26] If these results hold true across other forms of mind-body practices, it might be hypothesized that mindfulness practices such as meditation could also act differently in cancer cells and healthy cells, causing deterioration of cancer cells and improving the function of healthy cells.

A study by Dr. Linda E. Carlson, of the University of Calgary, has already explored the effects of meditation on telomerase levels and telomere length in patients with breast cancer. In comparing three groups of women with breast cancer, it was found that women who were diagnosed with cancer saw a rapid decline in the length of their telomeres (in healthy cells)—not from the cancer itself, but from the distress of the diagnosis.[27] Those who received no stress-reducing treatment continued to see declining levels of telomerase for the duration of the study.[28] However, women who received mindfulness training maintained their telomere length, in spite of the diagnosis of cancer.

This compelling finding has been corroborated by other research on the stressful effects of the diagnosis of cancer on immune and other systems functions. Just at a time when one needs all of their bodily systems functioning at their best for recovery, the emotional trauma of receiving a cancer diagnosis significantly impairs the body's survival mechanisms. This effect of trauma begins on the day that the diagnosis is received. However, studies also show that when people begin a meditation practice prior to receiving test results confirming cancer, they do not show these adverse reactions to the diagnosis itself.[29] Among people who were meditating when they received their diagnosis, even those who were positively diagnosed with cancer showed no effect on immune function or telomerase levels as a result of the diagnosis.

Meditation better prepares people for all of the stresses of life, including the life-altering upheaval that being diagnosed with cancer creates. In Dr. Carlson's study, patients who were taught to meditate after receiving a positive diagnosis for cancer maintained stable levels of telomerase and length of their telomeres![30] Meditation not only makes people feel more in control and able to manage a cancer diagnosis, but it also affects the very genes that are needed to become healthy again.

Oncologists would do well to prescribe meditation at the first moment that they begin to work with a patient. Scientists and epidemiologists would do well to explore the cultural phenomenon that leads to the profound anxiety and emotional trauma surrounding the diagnosis of cancer. It is beyond the scope of this book to go into detail about the factors that could create such a trauma, but I will mention that not all cultures experience this level of panic associated with the diagnostic label of cancer. Whether it is the life- threatening nature of the diagnosis or concern for the pending treatment, forebodingly referred to as "poison, slash, and burn," it is most likely both and more. Whatever it is, we need to recognize the culture of fear that we have created around diagnostic labels such as cancer, and address ways to change our attitude and relieve patients of iatrogenic trauma. As health care consumers, we can become empowered to recognize our own role and potential to use meditation and other mind-body practices for self-care and improved outcome. Given the wonderful side effects of meditation, there is no harm in anyone and everyone finding a practice that fits with their lifestyle.

Once again, I find science exploring the fascinating intersection of the connection between the mind and the body, the physical basis for psychological function, and the capacity for psychological phenomenon to change physical form. Understanding the interrelatedness of behavior, structure, and function is empowering us to regain control of both our mental and our physical health through self-care mindfulness practices. In realizing the impact of our behavior, we become the masters of our own health and well-being.

Relief from stress activated, short-term survival processes may point to the intersection between mindfulness practices and telomerase levels. At some point, we begin to wonder which comes first. Do the psychological processes alter the physical mechanisms, or do the physical states underlie the psychological outcomes? Here is where we need a conceptual change. Rather than thinking of mind and body as separate, as in one regulating the other, we can better understand the relationship between our behavior and physiology, or function and form, when we recognize that the mind is the body, and the body is the mind. They are one and the same thing. What is different is simply our perspective on our *selves*.

The mind *is* the body, and the body *is* the mind. They are not correlated, or even just related. They are the same. The experience of stress *is* the experience of the physical state of our body. Furthermore, the physical state of our being *is* the psychological experience that we describe. I recognize that this non-Descartian ideology is just a perspective. Yet it is a perspective that will help us to further understand the application of mindfulness in health care. It is the perspective that underlies the scientific basis that we demand for setting our health care standards. And it is the perspective that underlies all that we are learning about our capacity to self-regulate and to find our way back into the flow.

PART 2

Thalamic Gating: Expanding Consciousness with the Breath

Body Awareness

MAKE YOURSELF COMFORTABLE

BEGIN YOUR MEDITATION PRACTICE BY making yourself comfortable. This is a significant concept. Do it slowly, breaking down the process into baby steps. Before you move, start by noticing how your mind responds to the suggestion of making yourself comfortable. Notice what happens to your awareness as you consider your comfort. First, your awareness is directed away from the external world to the inside of your body. A quick scan of the body reveals places in the body that may not be comfortable. Then you respond to discovery of these places of discomfort by making visible, physical adjustments to relieve the discomfort and increase your sense of ease.

This whole process happens so quickly that we often make these adjustments, barely conscious or not even thinking about it. Perhaps you adjust your back or your legs. Perhaps you move cushions around and put a pillow behind you. Slow down and witness the mental processes as they interact with the physical. This practice of self-awareness and self-regulation is also a significant part of moving forms of meditation such as yoga and qigong. Yoga and qigong also involve the practice of finding or placing yourself in a unique physical posture and then consciously making physical adjustments to relieve constriction, free the breath, and become more comfortable.

In yoga, this sensation of flow or the movement within is referred to as prana. The practice of becoming aware of and moving prana is the practice of pranayama. In the practice of qigong, and also tai chi, the flow of energy and the breath is referred to as qi or chi. Becoming conscious of the sensation of flow is a key part of the practice of meditation. Whether you call it prana, qi, chi, energy, an electromagnetic field or the breath, it is all the same thing. It is a critical life force, characteristic of living things, and it moves. Position yourself during your meditation in such a way that you release restrictions to this flow by uncrossing your arms and legs, loosen your belt and your shoes, take off your glasses, and make your body comfortable. Comfort involves being able to sense the flow.

Initially this process of making yourself comfortable involves overt physical movement. But the process continues, as we make more and more subtle adjustments in the body. For example, at first you may appear to be physically moving, as you settle into your practice. Then you continue by making adjustments that are less visible. You may scan your body and notice that your shoulders are tense and so you relax your shoulders. Relaxing your shoulders is not necessarily a visible movement, but perhaps significantly improves your comfort. Similarly, you may check your jaw and facial muscles and allow them to relax. Next you may sense your neck and throat and make certain that they are relaxed and that you are breathing freely. Then check your chest and upper back. Notice how your ribs move gently with your breath. Take your time and let a sense of ease come over you. Continue to purposely scan your body, checking your comfort level and allowing the body to make further subtle adjustments. Notice your breath as you scan and how your body moves as it breathes. Continue to relax your arms, hands, facial expression, and legs. Use the breath as a guide to find areas of constriction and to make adjustments until the breath flows freely with ease throughout the entire body. Ultimately, with practice, you can cultivate such a profound state of ease, connection with the breath, and bodily comfort that you enter a blissful or euphoric state of being. So make yourself comfortable. Make physical adjustments, at first visible, and then subtle, all through the body until you find a sense of ease and a sensation of the flow of the breath.

Most of my students lie down at this point. Some people are concerned about falling asleep during meditation. The body puts a premium on what it needs, and if it needs sleep, it will take it. People in our society are generally chronically sleep-deprived, so if you fall asleep during meditation, you may be doing just what your body needs most to do. Meditating is even a good way to put yourself to sleep at night. By establishing a coherent state of mind as you prepare for your night's rest, you will sleep in that coherent state all night and awaken more refreshed and with a clearer mind. Eventually, as you become more rested, you will be able to stay awake during your practice. You may even enter a state of slow delta brain waves characteristic of deep sleep during your meditation practice, even though you are conscious and aware of your presence of mind. Yoga nidra meditation is the practice of entering this state of conscious yogic sleep. I have witnessed listening to myself softly snoring during my yoga nidra practice. I recognize that I am awake, but my body is so profoundly relaxed (comfortable) that my breathing slows, my throat relaxes, and I witness the rhythmic rumble of my breath. Ahh!

To Sit or Not to Sit. That Is the Question

If you want to sit upright while you are meditating, then do so in a comfortable way, with your seat elevated from the floor by a cushion or a chair, so that your hips and your legs can breathe and your circulation can flow. Or you may choose to stand. If standing, use a wide stance, one foot slightly in front of the other, knees softly bent, arms slightly elevated, palms facing down, as if you are standing in water and the arms are resting on the surface of the water. This stance is commonly used in the practice of qigong. I have stood like this for an hour at a time and find it an extremely satisfying way to meditate. Walking meditation is popular as well. Whichever position you choose, start your practice by making adjustments to become comfortable. As you practice awareness of the mental process you use to become comfortable, you gain a skill that you can use at any time, in any circumstance.

It may be controversial whether to sit, lie down, be still, move, ignore pain, or relieve it while meditating. I have heard many a student, and teacher, say that one *should* practice this way, or *should* practice that way. Given what research has shown, that what you practice is what you get, the only *should* is that you practice in a way that serves you. Practice in a way that empowers you to go deeper into the practice, to be in the flow, and to find meaning in your practice and your life. If you have an issue with *shoulds*, this can be explored in your practice as well.

Given that we are all different and have different needs and wants, the practice itself will inform you. What you are practicing is the ability to expand your consciousness—to become more aware of the experience of being. As your consciousness opens, you will become more aware of what is serving you, and what is not. I invite you to explore what works best for you, what makes you most comfortable. I have sat in lengthy, guided meditation practices where we were told to remain seated on the floor, knees crossed, upright, and though aches and pains may develop in the knees or low back, to stay seated and cope with the pain, simultaneously continuing with the mental practice and ignoring the pain. This is a doable practice that has its origins in the martial arts. As a technique for meditation, however, my research and experience suggests that it is not the best technique for the healing arts.

ATTENDING TO PAIN

I join my scientific and academic colleagues in intrigue with our mental capacity to ignore pain, though the cause of the pain and the pain itself persist. However, I do not concur with the practice of ignoring pain as a part of mindfulness practice in health care. Though it can be a useful skill when pain is unavoidable, it is contrary to the healing mechanisms of the body to ignore pain. Nor does ignoring pain align with the concepts of self- compassion and self-awareness characteristic of mindfulness practices.

In using meditation to facilitate optimal health, I recognize that people spend too much time ignoring physical pain and that this practice of sensory denial contributes greatly to chronic illness. We have the ability to filter out stimuli, as we do with white noise. We can ignore sensory information that is coming in through our senses, filtering it to a low hum in our subconsciousness. Again, to ignore sensory information is contrary to the meditative practice of expanding the consciousness. Studies examining the brain activity of monks who are long-term meditators show that they have increased cognitive awareness of environmental stimuli. The nerve pathways bringing information into the brain show increased activity. The brains of long-term meditators are more responsive to incoming sensory information than the brains of non-meditators. It is the outgoing information sent from the brain to the body that show decreased reactivity. While experienced meditators have increased situational awareness, they have decreased reactivity to irrelevant stimuli. They are consciously aware of what is going on, in a non-responsive state. Brain scans indicate that they are witnessing a broader range of experiences, yet are less reactive to them.

Long-term meditation practice gives practitioners increased capacity to regulate and control their reactivity to stimuli in the environment. Long-term meditators are freed from conditioning and thus are able to choose both how to react and whether or not to react. If you become aware that you are sitting in a way that is causing you pain, you may choose to move to alleviate the pain. Once you are comfortable, you may be still.

According to researchers Britta Holzel, Sara Lazar, and colleagues:

Framed in Western psychological terminology, one could say that non-reactivity leads to unlearning of previous connections (extinction and reconsolidation) and thereby to liberation from being bound to habitual emotional reactions. Since extinction mechanisms are thought to be supported by the experience of a state of relaxation while the individual encounters the feared stimuli,[31] *the relaxation component of meditation might serve to maximize the effects of the extinction process. Within the framework of mechanisms proposed in this study, self-compassion is presumably most related to emotion regulation as well as to the change in perspective on the self. The generation of feelings of kindness toward oneself in instances of perceived inadequacy or suffering (self-kindness) is an act of emotion regulation.*[32]

I often have children in my meditation classes who move and wiggle non-stop through the entire practice. My dad would say that they are "wearing out the inside of their clothing." After the practice, in spite of their incessant motion, such wiggle worms have reported profound experiences of altered states of bliss, floating, clarity, awe, and light. Wiggling is not a problem for the person who is wiggling, but more so for the observer. Who am I to judge whether you move or not. If no one else is bothered by your wiggling, do as you choose—wiggle or lie peacefully at ease. You are the best judge.

Thalamic Gating and Sensory Awareness

Medical research has shown that the practice of meditation can have two different types of effect on pain. One effect researchers measure is the effect of meditation on the ability to cope with pain. In coping with pain, practitioners report that the severity of the pain is unaffected; however, they are less bothered by the pain. Perhaps they are paying less attention to the pain, but when it is suggested to check, the intensity is still the same. Another measure evaluates whether the practice actually reduces the severity of the pain. With practices that affect this type of measure, there is less pain, and the measure of pain can actually be reduced to zero (no pain).

What we learn from this research using two different types of measures of pain is that some practices are effective in helping people to cope with pain, while others actually alleviate the pain. In coping with or managing pain, subjects rate their experience of pain *intensity* the same as before beginning the practice; however, they report that the pain causes less *interference* with mood and activities as a result of meditating. Other types of meditation practices, though, are effective in both coping and relieving pain. Using these types of practices, subjects report that there is less pain, or that there is no pain. The pain is gone. Once again, the outcome depends upon the type of practice. What you do is what you get. Some types of practice are allowing people to be better at ignoring or filtering out the pain; and some types of practices are actually resolving or healing the pain. What scientists are finding is that practices in which you are taught to ignore pain may make you better able to cope, but the pain itself is unresolved. Practices in which you attend to somatic (body) experiences of pain can actually relieve pain.

The ability to endure pain is a skill unto itself. Many cultures have rituals in which people are enamored with the skill of enduring pain. With practice people have accomplished feats of having their pectoral muscles pierced by rope so that they can hang for long periods of time and not complain of any pain. Facial piercing with long skewers is practiced as a ritual in Sufi traditions. Military soldiers are taught to endure pain and even torture without complaining. Kamikaze warriors went to their death, just as suicide bombers do today, in a trance of glory, without complaint.

One of the key roles of the brain is filtering out extraneous, incoming sensory stimulation. Many of the brain's functions are inhibitory, to block information from being processed. A familiar example of this is the phenomenon of filtering white noise or background noise that is constant and noninformative. We recognize white noise as something present, but our brains have somehow chosen not to pay attention to the noise. Indeed, a considerable amount of what the brain is doing is suppressing incoming information. The brain can in fact be trained to ignore pain.

We recognize two levels of information processing and storage, the conscious and the subconscious. You may not be thinking about the fact that there is a constant background noise, but when you reflect back on the circumstances, you may recall that you were subconsciously aware of an ongoing noise that you were ignoring. The information made it as far as your subconscious but was blocked or filtered from the consciousness.

The same is true with blocking sensations of pain from the consciousness. Theories abound about which parts of the brain are doing this filtering of information coming from the subconscious to the consciousness—and where exactly the subconscious resides and conscious mind begins. It is commonly assumed that the thalamus plays a major role in filtering incoming information from the sense organs and hindbrain to the cortex. This process of thalamic gating, choosing which information gets sent through to the frontal cortex for processing and which information gets suppressed to the realms of the subconscious, applies to all types of sensory input. Visual, olfactory, and tactile sensations are also filtered from our consciousness by the thalamus, depending upon the circumstances.

The brain somehow merges sensory information with the context in which it is being perceived. Dr. Dwayne Godwin and his colleagues are early proponents of the idea that this dynamic merging and processing of information may be occurring in the thalamus.[33]

The thalamus processes neural information coming from multiple sensory pathways. The thalamus has many specific nuclei that control the flow of sensory information to specific areas of the sensory cortex; for example, visual information is processed from the retina in the eye to the dorsal lateral geniculate of the thalamus, and from there to the visual cortex.

The thalamus is also known to play an important role in the modulation of pain. One of the sensory circuits processed is pain information ascending from the periphery of the body to the brainstem. Studies of the effects of pain on thalamic activation show that pain can cause changes in the biochemistry, gene expression, blood flow, and other response properties of thalamic neurons, suggesting that pain is indeed processed in the thalamus. The thalamus determines whether or not to transmit pain information into the higher cortex.

The Gate Control Theory of Pain, proposed by Melzack and Wall (1965), suggests that sensations of pain are able to be filtered from entering our conscious awareness.[34] They cite the example of dogs given a painful stimulus followed immediately by food. These dogs come to seek the painful stimulus, salivating in anticipation of food. The dogs are ignoring the pain and focusing on receiving the reward of food.

The concept of thalamic gating helps to explain the ability of warriors or others injured in a life-threatening situation to ignore pain and still function. When someone is in the heat of a battle for their life, if they become injured, they can't say, "Hold on a second, I've hurt myself; let me tend to this injury; it hurts." They can function better by ignoring the pain and remaining focused on the battle at hand. People often report that they didn't even notice that they were wounded until later when the threat was gone. The pain of the injury remains suppressed from the consciousness during the battle. Only under the right circumstances can awareness of the pain move into the consciousness, after the threat is removed.

The question that remains is, what drives the gating mechanisms of the thalamus? What causes the thalamus to keep sensory information from the consciousness, or let it through to the consciousness?

I propose that one of the driving factors that regulates the opening and closing of these thalamic gating mechanisms, and corresponding consciousness or lack thereof, is one's relative perspective of safety and threat. The gating of pain sensation closes during threat and opens, if we allow it to, during safety. Fear causes a narrowing of our focus; the focus narrows because the thalamus filters out what it believes to be extraneous information, for the purpose of survival. In particular, awareness of the body is blocked, and our brain is occupied with a narrower focus on external events. Intense trauma is even associated with shock in which tunnel vision, an extreme narrowing of the focus, can occur.

Relaxation, or a sense of safety, opens the thalamic gates and allows a broader range of information to enter our consciousness. When we feel safe, we can be more "open-minded," receiving more information from the subconscious into the consciousness, from the peripheral sensory projections, through the thalamus, and into the higher realms of processing in the brain. When we feel safe, we feel more present and more aware. These circumstances involve gradually relearning the experiences of safety, ease, and somatic sensing.

Brain mechanisms responsible for coordinating healing processes do not function as well when the thalamic gates are closed. Brain regulation of healing processes improves significantly once these gates open. The opening of the thalamic gates may allow information transfer to be reestablished between the conscious brain and the body. When the thalamic gates open to allow information from the subconscious (body) into the consciousness, the reverse may also be true; information flow is restored in both directions.

Somehow the sensation of truly being safe not only allows the consciousness to expand, but also facilitates the brain's ability to regulate healing in the body. Information flows both ways—from the body to the brain and from the brain to the body. Digestive function is restored. Hormones responsible for proper reproductive function are restored. Mineral corticoids are released to replenish the minerals needed for heart health, muscle function, and bone strength. Wound healing mechanisms are restored, growth hormones are released, and many other physiological functions necessary for long-term well-being are replete. The breath rate slows and becomes fuller, and the blood pressure lowers. When we are relaxed, the mechanisms that cause us to focus our awareness can also let go, so that more sensory information enters our consciousness. It is when we feel safe that we may begin to recognize signals from the body that there is a pain, a wound, or a blocked flow of energy. All of the research to date indicates that this act of opening our consciousness to receive messages from the body and letting the symptoms of pain arise into our awareness is related to the process of resolving the pain.

Focus is a key element of mindfulness meditation. Practiced attention to internal body sensations is a critical element of the practice of meditation for activating the healing response.[35] Awareness heals. When the consciousness expands, revealing the content of what was previously subconscious, the whole body becomes better integrated for long-term survival. We can again, smell the proverbial roses. At any time that you choose, the entire physical cascade of the relaxation response can be initiated by making yourself comfortable, breathing deeply, recognizing the feeling of safety, intentionally expanding the consciousness, and taking in the fullness of the experiences of being.

Deep, relaxed breathing also plays a role in thalamic gating mechanisms. When your brain is deficient in oxygen, the hypothalamus sends an alerting signal through the body, known as the stress response, or the fight-or-flight response. The brain cannot survive but for moments without oxygen, so when the brain senses an insufficiency of oxygen, this is cause for an extreme alerting of the activating system we call stress. Even a mild deficiency of oxygen will begin to activate the stress response. In addition to the familiar actions of the stress response, such as increased heart rate and blood pressure, the stress response triggers the thalamic gates to close and the brain to narrow its focus. Alternatively, when you breathe deeply, oxygen is absorbed into your bloodstream, richly oxygenating your blood. Oxygen is then carried through your circulatory system to every living cell in your body. When the brain receives a sufficiently rich supply of oxygen, it is recognized by the hypothalamus as a sign of safety. The relaxation response is elicited, the thalamic gates open, and consciousness expands (see Figure 1).

FIGURE 1: Shallow breathing is associated with the fear or threat response, which leads to closing of the thalamic gates in the brain. Closing the thalamic gates blocks information from the consciousness, keeping it in the subconscious. Blocking extraneous sensory information during times of fear or threat allows us to narrow and intensify our focus on only the most relevant information. Deep breathing is associated with feelings of safety. When we feel safe, the thalamic gates open, allowing more sensory information into the higher cortical areas of the brain associated with consciousness. As more sensory information is received into the consciousness, our awareness expands.

Processing Pain

We can sit at our desks all day and ignore the pain in our back. We can go for weeks and months and ignore a pain in our neck or shoulder. We can go for years enduring an uncomfortable work environment. And we can go a lifetime feeling stuck in a painful relationship. There is no denying that we can suppress, ignore, and tune out the experience of pain, to some extent. Some people have lived with pain for so long that they can't imagine what it would be like to be relieved of pain. Again, I am not to judge whether ignoring pain is good or bad. Such practices may have their reasons. It is certainly adaptive to be able to ignore pain when there is no way to be relieved of it, or when paying attention to a pain would be a distraction that might threaten your immediate survival.

The practice of ignoring pain, however, is not a practice that facilitates healing. Ignoring pain is what psychotherapists refer to as denial or resistance. Psychologists have a motto that *what we resist persists*. When an important message is trying to make its way from the subconscious into the consciousness, it will persist. Just like a child trying to get a parent's attention, a pain will continue to nag at you, eventually screaming if necessary to get your attention. And like paying attention to a child, paying attention to your pain can resolve the issue.

It continues to amaze me what we are able to do with intention using our brains. Resisting pain may cause it to persist, but attending to pain can resolve it. Recognizing the innate function of pain and attending to the sensation of pain allows you to activate the innate healing response. If what you want to do is heal your body, paying attention to and heeding the messages of pain is what will heal you.

The reason that we are able to experience pain is so that we can respond to it and make adjustments to create greater comfort. Pain is there for a reason. It tells us that something is wrong. It is adaptive to be able to sense pain, for without it, we would not survive.

When feeling pain is a threat to your immediate survival, you can ignore it. Once the battle is over, and there is no longer a threat, then you can take the time to focus on your pain and attend to your wounds. When we are safe, we find that our consciousness is able to recognize injuries that we may have received. Just as we are able to ignore pain when we are focused on a threatening situation, we are also able to attend to the pain once we feel safe. When we feel safe, the consciousness opens, and the messages from the body can be received.

My own research at the Veteran's Affairs Medical Center has shown that veterans in pain who begin a meditation program may initially show an increase in pain during the first couple of weeks of practice. It is during this time that soldiers report they feel safe enough to allow themselves to experience a pain that has been present all along, but which they tried to ignore. Over subsequent weeks of mindfulness practices, the veterans report that the pain subsides, and eventually after only eight weeks of practice, a number of veterans conclude that the pain is gone. This occurred in individuals who had had pain for months or years, and no other treatment had worked.[36] Indeed, a mindfulness practice of opening the consciousness and letting whatever is present come into awareness is a practice that restores the normal healing processes, and allows physical pain to heal.

Whether veteran or civilian, the practice of not allowing ourselves to feel safe can become a habit. We maintain a level of stress that narrows our focus and inhibits our consciousness. This habit blocks the brain's ability to regulate healing in the body. By breathing deeply, allowing ourselves to feel safe, and by relaxing into a more comfortable state, our consciousness expands and healing mechanisms are restored. We reconnect with the flow of consciousness from the body to the brain, and the brain to the body.

The concept of making yourself comfortable, of directing your consciousness inward and attending to your personal physical state is a significant part of the practice. Just as your mind will guide you to make adjustments to your back, your knees, or your shoulders to become more comfortable, it will continue to guide you in subtler adjustments that can potentially be used to relieve pain. Meditation practice is not a time to ignore pain. It may be a time to embrace it, or any other experience that arises in your awareness. By connecting your consciousness with the somatic experience of pain, you can release it. Pain simply moves through the consciousness on its way out. We have a choice: to continue to hold on to pain and resist letting go, or to attend within, breathe, release, and let go.

EXPANDING AND CONTRACTING THE CONSCIOUSNESS

Most of what the brain does is inhibitory. While we perceive the brain as "thinking," what the brain really is doing is filtering incoming information.

Irrelevant information stays in the subconscious. Relevant information gets transmitted to the consciousness.

The power of focus is the power of filtering incoming information, selectively attending to a narrower or wider range of potential input. When we focus more narrowly, we might miss a lot, but we get more detail about the subject of our experience. In a fight-or-flight situation, focus is useful. Nature gave us this capacity to narrow our focus so that we can function when our life is at stake. It is a crucial part of the flight-or-fight response.

The innate fight-or-flight response is accompanied by more rapid breathing and heartbeat, a change in hormonal and other physiological states of the body that include enhanced muscle function and other short-term survival mechanisms, and a decreased function of our long-term survival mechanisms. Reproductive hormones are put on hold. Mineral corticoids responsible for bone development and muscle (including heart) function are disrupted. Digestive processes are interrupted. Not only the brain, but also the entire body becomes focused on the momentary need to survive. The flow has been interrupted, and indeed we are focused on the moment. Time itself can seem to be altered by intense hyperfocus. Tunnel vision during a state of shock is an extreme example of the hyperfocus that can occur during a traumatic, life-threatening experience. It makes sense to use all of our personal resources for our short-term survival in a life-or-death situation, or we won't have use for these resources if we don't make it through that moment.

Once we are safe, our mental and physical mechanisms for long-term survival can come back into balance. Like adjusting the zoom on a camera lens, we can expand the range of incoming information. We can expand our perspective. The key is recognizing when we are safe.

Consider a time when you have looked out across a broad expanse of landscape, with the horizon off at a distance. In the calm of a peaceful moment, you can take in a broad perspective of the horizon. If there is a sudden movement on the landscape, your attention will be instantly drawn to a sharper focus on that which is moving. Non-synchronous or abrupt movements are an indication of potential danger. The zoom on your lens of observation will go from wide to narrow in an instant, limiting your perspective but giving you more detail about the point of focus. Once your cortex has processed the information and determined that there is no threat and you are safe, then the zoom will again expand.

Unlike abrupt, asynchronous movements, continual or rhythmic sensations are calming. Watching waves at the beach, observing a murmuration of a flock of birds, or listening to rhythmic sounds, like the beating of a heart, are all soothing and allow the consciousness to expand. The ebb and flow of the breath is a soothing rhythmic point of focus to use to get in the flow during the practice of meditation.

There is a lot of information being received into and stored in the subconscious. As you practice meditation and become more acclimated to feelings of comfort, safety, and ease, the consciousness will continue to open and the contents of the subconscious will continue to be revealed to you. It is because mindfulness practices can access what was previously in the subconscious, and release it into the consciousness, that mindfulness serves as the foundation for behavioral change.

CHAPTER 6

Mindfulness: The Foundation for Behavioral Change

THE EVOLUTION OF BEHAVIOR

Cell-to-cell communication serves as the basis for functional coordination between unicellular organisms, as well as between cells in multicellular organisms.

-Felix Scholkmann, Daniel Fels, and Michal Cifra
Cell-to-cell communication: Current views and future perspectives (2013) [37]

THE FIRST COURSE THAT I ever taught at American University was a class on The Evolution of Behavior, pleasantly combining my interests in genetics and neuroscience. It was really a course on the evolution of the nervous system, since behavior can be described as a function of the underlying physical system. As the physical structures evolved, the behavioral potential of the animal changes as well. What we have learned from the science of mindfulness is that our behavior can also change the physical structure of our brains. Both our genes and our behavior affect the structure and function of our brains. Since mindfulness practices can alter both the structure and function of our brains, mindfulness underlies our potential for behavioral change. To understand how mindfulness practices facilitate changes in our brain and our behavior, let's take a brief look at how the nervous system evolved.

The nervous system evolved as a communication network for all of the various cells in the body. This internal communication network is a way for the right side of the body to respond to something that is happening on the left side; or a way for the inside of the body to know what is happening on the outside of the body. In the case of more complex animals, this internal communication system is a way for the brain to know what is happening throughout the body, to integrate those sensations, and to coordinate activities accordingly. Your eyes can see a chair, and your body knows to respond by sitting in it. You could just as well end up on the floor, but your brain is able to integrate what you see with your eyes, and coordinate what you do with your body so you end up in the chair.

The earliest communication system to evolve was a network of somewhat random sensory cells that might touch and overlap and stimulate each other in the way that sea-dwelling sponges communicate with each other. Eventually, individual nerve cells evolved that could communicate with each other through a flow of electrochemical events. An electrical charge flows from one cell to another, altering the electro-chemical state of nearby cells. Since electromagnetic fields flow readily through water, the ability to sense and respond to electromagnetic shifts readily evolved as a means of intra-organism and intracellular communication. Even primitive sea-dwelling animals could easily communicate through this electromagnetic sensing mechanism.

As the cellular structure of animals has grown more complex, so has the structure of the nervous system. A more recent advancement in the evolution of the nervous system was the development of ganglia, clusters of neurons that regulate activities in specific regions of the body. Most ganglia are located along the spine in humans and other vertebrate animals.

Each ganglion regulates activities called reflexes in a specific area of the body. Reflexive actions can occur on their own, before neural impulses even have time to make it all the way to the brain. Ganglion regulation of reflexes allows reflexes to happen very quickly.

Reflexive actions are hard-wired to the ganglion from birth. Our genes dictate reflexive behaviors because they are critical to our survival. We call these reflexive behaviors instincts because they occur in all individuals of a species in response to a specific stimulus, and appear to be pre-programmed in the genes.

All animals have a multitude of reflexive behaviors, behaviors that don't need input from the brain. Reflexes are fast acting survival mechanisms. They don't require thinking or deciding. They can happen before the brain gets involved. Tap the palm of a baby, and the hand will reflexively close. Make a sudden loud noise, and most people will jump in response. The blink of your eyes happens reflexively in response to a gust of air.

Certain reflexes are critical to our survival. Indeed, it may be that all reflexes are critical; that's why they exist. The cycle of breathing is a reflex. Go under water and you reflexively stop breathing; come up and you reflexively inhale. Your circulatory system has a reflexive mechanism as well. Tap a vein, and it reflexively contracts. The heartbeat has a reflexive mechanism. Scare it and your heart reflexively contracts, or "skips a beat". Exhale and it reflexively calms and expands. Many bodily functions happen reflexively. Reflexive actions are rules to live by, literally; the very foundation of our behavioral repertoire.

One such reflex is the knee-jerk reaction that occurs when the doctor taps the patellar tendon in your knee. The patellar reflex is coordinated by local ganglion in the lumbar spine (L3). The patellar reflex does not need the brain to cause it to happen. However, information about this action is relayed to the brain. In certain circumstances, the brain is capable of overriding reflexive actions. In our awareness, if we so choose, we can inhibit the patellar reflex and keep the leg from swinging in response to the doctor's hammer. By choosing whether to allow a reflex or to inhibit it, the brain is able to coordinate reflexes with other incoming sensory information.

The brain first evolved as a sort of central ganglion. While each ganglion in an animal coordinates the activity of a specific region of its body, the brain can integrate activity of all of the various ganglion, resulting in more coordinated behavior. The brain adds another layer of potential to the complexity of behavior. We can see from the behavior and function of the earliest forms of brains that the primary function of this centralized nervous system was to inhibit some reflexes while allowing others. The brain is associated with the ability to "choose" how to behave by prioritizing or blocking reflexive behaviors.

Behavior is fundamentally a multitude of reflexive activities, with some of these reflexive activities being selectively inhibited, while others are selectively allowed. At any given time, events in the environment may be stimulating ganglion to activate reflexive behaviors, but the brain is overriding these reflexes, controlling, coordinating and fine-tuning behavior. In contrast to reflexive behavior regulated by the ganglion on the spine, the brain learns to inhibit reflexes, giving rise to different behavioral options. Learned behaviors appear to be acquired as a result of conscious exploration, rather than genetic programming. Whereas reflexes are automatic, learning gives each individual the opportunity to develop their own way of responding to the environment.

Using the brain to inhibit reflexes allows us to control our behavior, changing it to suit the circumstances. Meditation is a way to access the brain's potential for reflex control. Mindfulness practices are an exercise in cultivating and coordinating our reflex control.

Reflex Inhibition: The Neural Basis of Behavioral Control

Most of what the brain does is inhibitory. While we perceive the brain as "thinking" what the brain really is doing is filtering incoming information. Irrelevant information stays in the subconscious. Relevant information gets transmitted to the consciousness. When information about a reflex gets transmitted through the thalamic gates to the consciousness, we are able to control our reflexes. When the gates are closed, we are acting reflexively and are not able to self-regulate. Control is achieved by choosing to allow or inhibit a programmed reflex.

When we pick up something burning hot, there is a reflex that would have us drop it. However, if we are holding a hot pot and there is a child nearby, the brain can override the reflex, so that we can place the hot pot down safely away from the child.

The brain mechanism of inhibiting action is why the proverbial chicken runs around the barnyard when it loses its head - because without the brain, all reflexive actions are firing randomly at the same time. In mindless unawareness, we lose the ability to control our reflexive behaviors. We act out. We feel out of control. We don't know why we are behaving as we are, and we feel helpless to change.

We are all well aware of or conscious of our breath. Therefore, we can easily learn to control our breathing. We can intend to inhale or exhale, and the conscious brain controls the breathing reflex. The brain can also learn to coordinate other vital functions, as long as we can bring conscious awareness to these experiences. In mindfulness meditation, the simple practice of bringing the focus of your awareness to your internal experiences of your body enhances your ability to regulate the functions of the body. Wherever you focus your attention, there will be growth in the region of the brain that regulates that function, and there will be enhanced ability for self-regulation and self-control. Focus on your breath, and you will begin to breathe more deeply and calmly.

The brain's gift of response-inhibition allows multiple factors in the environment to be taken into consideration in determining the response. For example, if there is a noise, pay attention to it. If the noise is constant, begin to ignore or block attention to it, as with white noise. In mindful awareness, we can sense these reflexive urges. With practice in attending to the sensations of these urges, we grow neural pathways along these reflex arcs to cultivate coordination. We are able to self-regulate through reflex-inhibition. Neuroplasticity allows us to cultivate coordination of many facets of the body, sometimes permitting reflexive behaviors, and sometimes inhibiting them. Conscious coordination of reflexive behaviors gives us a choice in how we respond.

Cultivating Coordination

If consciousness is a product of thalamocortical activity, it is the dialogue between the thalamus and the cortex that generates subjectivity.

-György Buzsáki and Rafael H. Llinas
Temporal Coding in the Brain (2012) [38]

The brain has several different inhibitory mechanisms. First it can block sensory information from even entering the consciousness, as I've described with thalamic gating. (These "Memories" may then stay locked in the subconscious of the physical body.) When the thalamic gates are closed to sensory input, the brain cannot coordinate a response to it. Reflexive behaviors activated by sensory stimulation will occur, uninhibited and uncontrolled. In this state, we are functioning on reflexes. We notice how we are behaving, but feel at a loss to control what is "happening to us". This state can feel exhausting and out of control. We say things like, "You made me do it"; or, "I couldn't help myself".

A second type of inhibition happens when information is able to make it into the consciousness. When the thalamic gates are open to incoming sensory experience, the cortex is able to send messages back out to the periphery of the body to inhibit reflexive actions and regulate behavior. When the gates are closed we have no choice. We are stuck. When they open, by attending to the sensation, we have the option to respond, or simply allow. Mindfulness is the foundation for behavioral change because mindfulness practices open the thalamic gates to let sensory information into the consciousness where it can be processed, and where we have the choice in whether and how to respond. Consciousness cultivates coordination. Through a process of integrating multiple sensory bits of information, the brain is able to coordinate appropriate responses to potentially variable circumstances. Coordination of our behavior and function gives us the ability to choose how we respond to our environment.

Given the many reflexive behaviors that can occur at any moment (picture the chicken running around), the option to dampen any number of reflexes using the consciousness may be a great relief. The more reflexes we choose to still, the more still we feel. Open-minded experiential consciousness is the basis for the stillness that we seek in our practice.

Sensate awareness is what mindfulness practitioners refer to as "being in the here and now". There are a multitude of sensory opportunities. Mindfulness is an invitation for sensate experiences to enter the consciousness. Sitting in quiet reflection of the sensate experience of being requires very little reaction.

In the process of allowing sensation in through the gates of consciousness, the brain has the potential to inhibit extraneous reflexive activity. For humans, the ability to coordinate reflexive behaviors gives us a sense of control. This accounts for why researchers today find that mindful self-awareness is associated with a greater sense of self-control and self-regulation.[39]

I recently had a student in my online meditation community describe a near-miss collision with another car. Afterwards, the thing that amazed her the most was that she had no visceral or other autonomic response to the event. She remained calm and steady as she drove around the oncoming car. Her reflexive startle response did not occur, even in this extreme, life-threatening situation. She explained that through meditation, she is able to stay grounded and centered, feeling in control of her emotions and behavior. Through her practice, her brain has developed pathways into the body to inhibit the reflexive startle response, giving her a sense of serenity and self-control.

OPENING THE MIND LEADS TO TRANSFORMATION AND BEHAVIORAL CHANGE

The important thing is not to stop questioning. Curiosity has its own reason for existing.

-Albert Einstein (1879-1955)

I define meditation as the practice of being in a state of curious awareness. Curiosity is the mental process of inviting the thalamic gates to open, to allow experience to arise, unfettered by fear. Before children learn rules for closing their minds, they are curious. In our meditation practice, we allow these gates to reopen. By sitting in a mindful state, in curious awareness of the experiences of being, we can let go of reflexive behavioral patterns. We have the opportunity to unlearn old ways of being that are no longer functional, and discover new ways of self-regulating our behavior. Herein lies the potential for behavioral change.

Clinical research shows that people who practice mindfulness meditation experience major transformations in their physical and mental health. The practice of meditation has significant effects on the biochemistry and the structure and function of the brain. The simple practice of intentionally opening the mind – the thalamic gates to consciousness – by sitting in a state of curious awareness, and attending curiously to the breath and other experiences that arise leads to potentially significant transformation.

Mindfulness is the foundation for behavioral change, because it allows for changes in the rules regarding what information gets through the thalamic gates, and how that information is processed into action. Mindfulness opens our minds and the potential for new truths. In opening the mind, it expands the consciousness. Mindfulness practices enhance the brain's capacity to coordinate the multiple functions of the body, allowing healing and transformation.

THE KEY TO HIGHER CONSCIOUSNESS: THE HYPOTHALAMUS

If the gate to the consciousness is the thalamus, the key to unlocking the gates of the thalamus is a small gland that lies just below it called the hypothalamus. The hypothalamus is an alerting system for activating body-wide responses, like those involved in the fight-or-flight response, also known as the stress response. It also regulates sleep and consciousness. Activation of the hypothalamus invites us to focus more intensely. The hypothalamus receives information from the body, through the brainstem, and sends instructions to other major glands in the body and the brain. Since it rests nestled below the thalamus, the thalamus is quickly alerted by the hypothalamus. When the hypothalamus is activated by stress or fear, it informs the gating mechanisms of the thalamus, closing gates and blocking incoming information.[40] Anything potentially distracting is blocked, limiting incoming sensory information to only the most important sources. Sensations of pain or digestion are blocked. Incoming information about immune function or inflammation is blocked. Sensations of pleasure, ease or joy are blocked from the higher levels of consciousness. When the hypothalamus is activated, only the subject or our most intense focus is permitted through the gates to our consciousness.

Are You Okay? Are You Breathing?

I like to compare the hypothalamus to an overly concerned mother, constantly asking, "Are you okay?", "Is something wrong?", "What's going on?", "How are you now?" Sometimes it seems that the slightest thing can set it off. Left to its own devices, it can work itself into a tizzy. And yet, there is a way to soothe it and reassure it that all is well. What the hypothalamus wants is for you to exhale.

One of the primary concerns of the hypothalamus is the presence of too much carbon dioxide. When we hold our breath, carbon dioxide levels in the blood begin to rise. Too much carbon dioxide in the blood from shallow breathing or holding the breath increases the acidity in the blood (acidosis). Acidosis activates the hypothalamus, which then alerts the thalamus to narrow its focus.[41, 42] When we exhale, we release carbon dioxide. Intentionally breathing deeply, or allowing the full-bodied breathing reflex to occur uninhibited, lowers the acidity of the blood and actually soothes the hypothalamus.[43] This relaxation effect is why the sigh of relief feels so good. The exhale literally soothes the brain. Exhaling happens naturally when we are conscious of the breath.

Understanding of the role of the breath suggests that there are at least two important ingredients to the mindfulness practice: the exhale, which is the key to unlocking the thalamic gates, and curious awareness of sensate experiences, which opens the thalamic doors to consciousness. The exhale serves as a tool for soothing the hypothalamus and unlocking the thalamic gates. Once unlocked, curious awareness is an invitation to the thalamic gates to open, inviting sensate awareness to arise. As sensate experience arises, the brain has access to coordinating and regulating our behavior.

Those who may be frustrated at initial attempts to meditate may do well to begin their practice by focusing on the exhale for a while. Spend some time getting excess carbon dioxide out of the blood-stream before settling in to sensate awareness. After you have done the practice this way a few times, you will be able to settle more directly into experiential awareness, and beyond.

The hypothalamus, that great perpetrator of fear, holds the keys to our consciousness. When we live in fear, we lose access to the healing power of our consciousness. Attending to the breath soothes our fears, opens our mind, and gives us the keys to consciousness.

How Mindfulness Heals

The ability of the body to heal is remarkable. Stories abound about people healing, and many have reported their own recovery from what we call chronic conditions. I myself have recovered from several diagnoses of chronic diseases, including a diagnosis of fibromyalgia, as well as seizures that I suffered from a severe head trauma. In both cases I was told that these were lifelong conditions. I was handed prescriptions including opiate pain-killers, benzodiazepine sedatives, anti-depressants and anti-epileptic drugs to help me cope. Instead, I recovered.

The scientific literature is now full of clinical trials showing that mindfulness practices are able to alleviate clinical conditions, including conditions ranging from chronic pain to heart disease, inflammation to depression, PTSD, cancer and more.[44] Studies show that wounds heal faster, pain rescinds, cholesterol improves, blood sugar rebalances and insulin function improves, inflammation is relieved, mood improves, sleep improves. Indeed, every measure of health that has been studied has been found to improve, every risk factor for heart disease, every diagnostic component of diabetes improves with meditation.[45] Cancer survival rates increase. Telomerase levels increase, lengthening telomeres and putting our strands of DNA back together, literally reversing the aging process. Mindfulness exercises have a powerful impact on every measurable dimension of our well-being.

After decades of clinical research on mind-body practices, we have a much clearer picture of how mindfulness heals the body. Healing involves cultivating coordination of the brain's ability to regulate bodily functions. We develop coordination of the body when we learn as toddlers to walk. We improve our coordination when we learn to dance, ride a bicycle, or other exercise. The conscious brain also coordinates heart function, digestion, inflammation, pain and healing. Every function in the body requires the brain to regulate that function, including the healing responses that keep our body functioning properly. The conscious brain coordinates the healing response. Meditation accesses the conscious brain's ability to heal by improving coordination of the healing processes.

CHAPTER 7

Ooh, Las Vagus Nerve! How to Control Your Behavior

NON-JUDGMENTAL AWARENESS

WHEN WE SIT IN MEDITATION aware of the sensations arising from our body, information flows two ways between the body and the brain. Incoming information flows towards the brain along what we call afferent nerve pathways. These pathways bring information into the brain from all over the body; every sound, sight, or touch, every sensation, every feeling, comes in along these afferent paths. When you are aware that a bird is singing, that information is flowing from your eardrums through afferent nerves, to your brain.

Information from the brain to the body flows out along efferent nerve pathways. Efferent nerve pathways, send information from the brain to the muscles, organs and elsewhere, even the bones, coordinating every function that occurs in the body. The brain coordinates muscle movements so that individual muscles can work together in unison performing all of our movements like dancing, driving, or threading a needle. When you decide to get up and walk across the room, your brain sends messages out through efferent nerves to coordinate the muscle actions involved in standing up and walking, coordinating this action with the afferant sensations that it is receiving.

During meditation, sensate experience comes in to the brain through the afferent pathways. Simultaneously, the brain has access to the efferent pathways to send messages regulating and coordinating reflexive behaviors. When the brain has access to the body, many unnecessary reflexive behaviors can be blocked by the conscious mind. In this way, cultivating coordination of bodily reflexes, dampening those reflexes that are unnecessary and allowing those that are, cultivates a sense of internal stillness that grows with our practice. Being in a state of curious awareness cultivates coordination of greater peace and equanimity.

The Physiological Basis of Compassion: The Vagus Nerve

The mind has great influence over the body, and maladies often have their origin there.

-Molière (1622-1673)

A single nerve called the Vagus nerve carries information between the sense organs and the brain. Often considered the neural basis for the mind-body connection, the vagus nerve is the longest cranial nerve pathway in the body. The vagus nerve extends from the brainstem at the base of the skull, behind the ears, and down the sides of the neck along the carotid artery. It then passes across the chest and down through the abdomen connecting with all of the major organs. In addition to carrying sensory information from the organs that we traditionally think of as sense organs, such as the eyes and the ears, it also carries apparently sensate information from all of the organs in the body, including the heart and the gut.

The heart is well-known for its vagal connections with the brain. While mindfulness practices can create visible effects in the brain that are measurable using electroencephalography and magnetic resonance imaging, we are not able to measure shifts in the electric field or magnetic resonance in the vagus nerve, since it is a much more diffuse structure. Instead, we measure heart-rate variability to imply that the vagus nerve is functioning. Since the brain regulates heart rate via the vagus nerve, high heart rate variability suggests that the vagus nerve is functioning effectively. When the brain can sense what the heart is doing and can promptly coordinate changes in the heart rate as needed to maintain homeostasis in the body, we have good vagal tone.

There are many ways to enhance vagal tone, and mindfulness meditation is key among them. When we practice somatic sensing, we are intentionally activating the vagus nerve, inviting the thalamic gates to open and inform the consciousness of sensory experience. We can become aware of sensate experiences arising from the heart. Compassion-based practices invite the consciousness to focus on the heart and coordinate the sensation of expanding the heart. These exercises activate the vagus nerve, improve heart-rate variability, and can change our emotional status.

According to Dacher Ketlner, Director of the Social Interaction Laboratory at the University of California, Berkley, "People who have high vagus nerve activation in a resting state ... are prone to feeling emotions that promote altruism – compassion, gratitude, love and happiness." Ketlner's research also suggests that people who practice feeling emotions of altruism, compassion, gratitude, love and happiness may be able to improve vagus nerve activation and heart rate variability. These are the emotional labels for the feelings that we sense with our heart.

Activation of the heart is the very definition of activation of the vagus nerve. As with any form of exercise for cultivating coordination, a little practice goes a long way. In your practice, explore with curious awareness the sensations of your heart, and let that sensation meld with the greater sensate experience of being.

Gut Instincts: I Have a Gut Feeling...

It is now evident that the bidirectional signaling between the gastrointestinal tract and the brain, mainly through the vagus nerve, the so called "microbiota–gut–vagus–brain axis," is vital for maintaining homeostasis and it may be also involved in the etiology of several metabolic and mental dysfunctions/disorders. Here we review evidence on the ability of the gut microbiota to communicate with the brain and thus modulate behavior.[46]

-Augusto J. Montiel-Castro, Rina M. Gonzales-Cervantes, Gabriela Bravo-Reuiseco and Gustavo Pacheco-Lopez
The Microbiota-Gut-Brain Axis: Neurobehavioral Correlates, Health and Sociality (2013)

If feeling with the heart is the Sixth Sense, then feeling with the gut is yet another. The way that the vagus nerve processes sensations from the body towards the sensory cortex of the brain suggests that visceral sensations are also important sensory information that influence our mood and our cognitions. Researchers have discovered that the digestive system also has sensory pathways through the vagus nerve bringing sensory information to the consciousness.[47,48] Referred to as the "microbiota-gut-vagus-brain reflex arc", we now know that the bacteria in our gut communicate with the brain.

Since 2014, there has been an explosion of interest in the gut-brain relationship, with headlines like "Gut microbes and the brain: paradigm shift in neuroscience"[49], "The role of the microbiome in central nervous system disorders"[50] and "The impact of gut microbiota on brain and behavior: implications for psychiatry".[51] As I write this, the National Institutes of Health are funding numerous research programs further exploring the role of gut biota in communicating with our brain, and regulating our behavior and health.

Communication between the gut and the brain is bidirectional. Gut bacteria affect our behavior and mood by sending sensory information via the vagus nerve to the brain. The brain responds to these messages by modulating our blood sugar, our metabolism and our immune response among other effects. When we close our consciousness to visceral sensations, we lose the ability to coordinate these processes. Inflammation runs rampant, blood sugar is unregulated, and metabolic functions fail. When we open our consciousness during mindfulness meditation to sensations of the body, including sensations arising in the gut, we re-establish this mind-body connection and the capacity to regulate these essential functions. The concept of having a "gut feeling" implies the ability to experience feelings in the gut. Mindfulness implies attending to these feelings. During your meditation practice, attend to sensations arising in your belly. As you breath, and let your mind explore sensations arising from within, attend to any gut feelings you may experience.

MINDFULNESS AND THE "INFLAMMATORY REFLEX ARC"

Not only is sensory information from the heart and the gut transmitted to the brain through the vagus nerve, we also know that information about inflammation is part of a vagal reflex arc. According to Kevin Tracey, Director of the Feinstein Institute and Professor and President of the Elmezzi Graduate School of Molecular Medicine in Manhasset, New York, "The nervous system reflexively regulates the inflammatory response in real time, just as it controls heart rate and other vital functions."[52] Inflammation is a reflex that the conscious brain can control.

Earlier studies have shown that meditation reduces inflammation and improves immune function, but no one knew how or why. I suggest that body sensing improves vagal tone or the mind-body connection with inflammatory processes, and allows the brain to coordinate inflammation. The brain differentially responds to good bacteria and pathological bacteria – inciting an inflammatory attack on bad bacteria. Furthermore, breath focused mindfulness exercises may also soothe the hypothalamus. Quelling hypothalamic activity both relieves the stress response and unlocks the thalamic gates allowing the brain to access and coordinate the inflammatory reflex.

In a study of mice in which the inflammatory reflex pathways of the vagus nerve were cut, inflammation became out of control. The brain no longer had access to sensing or regulating the inflammation. Similarly, when the thalamic gates are closed, the brain does not have access to regulate the inflammatory reflex. What these findings suggest is that breathing and body sensing cultivate the capacity to modulate immune function and inflammation by enhancing vagal tone and opening the thalamic gates into the consciousness.

Inflammation is often associated with pain, so as you begin this process, you may first open to the experience of pain. However, as I've already described, connecting the conscious brain with the sensation of pain may be the element of the practice that allows healing. Depending on the amount of pain, professional guidance may be needed. In all cases, one should proceed gradually and gently. As you invite compassion and self-caring into your practice, you open your heart, and the vagal pathways into the body, easing and enhancing the process.

I Feel It in My Bones

Even our bones have been found to communicate via the vagus nerve with the brain, suggesting that we can sense qualitative experiences within our bones.[53] Neurohormones secreted by our bones communicate with the brain, sending information that affects our appetite, our metabolism, insulin function and mood. During physical exercise, we activate newborn bone cells called osteoblasts. These new bone cells release a hormone (lipocalin-2) that works in the brain to suppress our appetite. Other neurohormones, like serotonin, are also regulated by our bones, sending information to our brains, changing the signals that the brain sends back out to the rest of our body, affecting our mood and our health. No part of the body is immune from regulation by the brain, or from the potential for our conscious awareness. Curious awareness of the experience of being may reveal to us far more than we are expecting. However, science has documented that our hearts, our digestive system, inflammatory processes throughout our body, and even our bones, provide sensory information which during times of deep relaxation and opening of the Thalamic Gates, is available to the conscious brain. Furthermore, as we access these deeper felt-senses of our being, we cultivate the capacity to coordinate these processes, and render healing and well-being to our experience of life. Sit back, breathe deeply, and notice the feeling deep within the marrow of your bones. Spend some time there, in curious awareness, noting the feelings that may arise.

CHAPTER 8

The Breath

FOCUS ON THE BREATH: WHY BREATHE?

Because no cancer cell exists, the respiration of which is intact, it cannot be disputed that cancer could be prevented if the respiration of the body cells would be kept intact.[54]

-Otto Warburg
The Metabolism of Tumors in the Body (1927)

THERE ARE SEVERAL REASONS WHY the breath is a useful point of focus in your meditation practice. One convenience of using the breath as a point of focus for beginning meditation is that as long as it matters, the breath is always immediately available. In those tense moments in life, like when driving a car and another car suddenly swerves into your lane and your heart begins pounding with the surge in adrenalin, you do not need to pull out a candle and find a match in order to focus and calm down. You can simply shift your focus to your breathing and quell the surge of adrenalin. During a stressful meeting, you do not need to start chanting or singing "Ohm." You can simply shift your focus inward to notice that you are breathing, and the familiar sensation of peacefulness settles over you. With continued practice, you may even discover that peaceful focus becomes your response to what others may term "stressful." With practice, shifting the focus to the breath and away from whatever else is at hand, becomes a conditioned response to stressful situations. Practice

76

allows this reflexive relaxation response to come quickly and helps to cultivate mindfulness in the broader context of one's life. Once this response is conditioned, reflection on the breath can be used at any time, in most any situation, to create a sense of inner ease, calm, or peace.

Another benefit to using the breath as the focal point for beginning your meditation practice is that breathing is an intrinsic stimulus for the relaxation response. In the privacy of quiet reflection, observance of the breath and the many qualities of the breath has a physiological effect that is palpably calming. Just as intentional smiling can begin the release of serotonin and the accompanying sensations of happiness, intentional breathing similarly shifts us from the realm of the stress response to the realm of the relaxation response. The relaxation response is incompatible with the stress response. You cannot have both responses simultaneously. They are opposites on the same continuum. As you intentionally focus on your breath, you short circuit the cascade of hormones that trigger stress, and you shift your body into relaxation mode, releasing waves of hormones associated with pleasurable feelings of relief and ease.

Using your breath as the focus of your meditation practice can also have beneficial effects on the brain. As the brain receives oxygen, it registers safety; it is easier for it to calm its busy activity. In meditation, I liken thoughts in the head to little clouds floating across a broad expanse of blue sky. Your breath is like a gentle breeze that carries the clouds across the sky. They move across the blue sky carried on the breeze of your breath. Sometimes more clouds arise, and sometimes thoughts, like clouds in the sky, evaporate in the light of sunshine. Simply notice your breath as you might notice a breeze in a clear, sunny blue sky. With this opening and clearing, you have made room in your consciousness for other experiences of the sensations of being.

As we shift our brain's attention from its multitude of tasks to a single intended point, such as the breath, and then let go of that point of focus and allow our senses to be permeated with the experience of being, the miracle of the meditation practice continues to unfold. As our conscious-ness opens and our awareness expands, we take note of the experiences that arise.

On an occasion when I was speaking to a group of university profes-sors on the topic of "Stress Management," they pleaded with me to sug-gest something to quickly help them to deal with stress. I suggested that they simply begin breathing deeply. "No" they said, shaking their heads. "Seriously. We want a tool we can use to help us cope with stress now." Again, I repeated, "Breathe deeply," this time instructing them to do it now. A few of them started to breath more deeply. And others continued to try to explain their frustration at this apparently difficult question. They expected it to be a difficult and complicated exercise. "No," they thought, "success can only be gained through hard work. The solution to such a major problem as the stress in my life cannot be easy. It has got to be hard or complicated." Well, think again. If we are going to create ease in our lives, by definition, it has got to be easy. Doing what we interpret as hard work is not going to create a sense of ease. Clearly it has got to appear to be easy, feel easy, and ultimately *be* the sensation of ease, in order to create the experience of ease in our lives.

What is one of the easiest things that you can think of to do? Try breathing.

Seriously, breathe deeply now. Take five intentional deep breaths and notice how you feel. Then do that the next time you notice a sense of "stress" or any other unpleasant feeling in your body, and notice any shift in your experience of being.

How did we get to be a culture of people who brag about how stressed out we are? I once saw a poster over a person's desk that said, "I don't work 9 to 5, I work crisis to crisis." First, why would we brag about this obvious lack of self-control, and, secondly, why would some manufacturer choose to print and market such a poster to the public? Because being stressed-out is a trend. When my friends ask me how I'm doing and I reply "Great! Loving life!", sometimes they grunt with dismay that I'm just not with the program. It seems like we check in with each other to validate ourselves that we are all equally disgruntled. Be aware that when you find this equanimity and learn to cultivate peace, joy, or any experience of your choosing, you are setting a new trend in our culture. Rather than being seduced by the sympathy that we shower upon each other for being overworked and overwhelmed, use the sense of comfort as a true guide to staying in the flow in your life. It is safe to be comfortable, and it is comfortable to be safe.

How to Breathe

> *The prime cause of cancer is the replacement of the respiration of oxygen in normal body cells by a fermentation of sugar. All normal body cells meet their energy needs by respiration of oxygen, whereas cancer cells meet their energy needs in great part by fermentation.*[55]
>
> -Otto Warburg
> *The Metabolism of Tumours in the Body* (1927)

To respire is to breathe; to take in breath, or inspire, and to let go of the breath, or expire. The roots of this word are *re*, as in to do again, and *spiri*, Latin for spirit. As you breathe, notice the ebb and flow sensation of the breath, like waves at the beach, a constant soothing motion that flows through the entire body.

Notice the sensation of the inhale. What does it feel like to inspire? There is a reason for the two meanings of the word inspire, meaning both to breathe in and to take in creative energy. Feel the sensation as you inspire. We do not *intend* to inspire, we *become* inspired; we receive inspiration. The verb is passive. Allow the body to receive the breath and to become breathed.

We can intend to breathe in a certain way, such as holding the breath or commanding an inhale or an exhale, but only for so long before some greater force comes along and causes us to get back in the flow. Such it is with life. We can intend our lives in a certain direction, but only for so long before some greater force comes along and through whatever drama is necessary to release our resistance causes us to get back in the flow.

If we are passive recipients of the breath, what is our role in the process? Our role is to be witness to the phenomenon of being breathed. Again, most of what the brain does is inhibitory. Let your cognitive processes get out of the way and simply exist as the witness of your body being breathed. Sense the phenomenon. It is a remarkable experience, worthy of exploring in detail.

Notice the moment at the top of the breath—that instant when the inhale begins to become an exhale. Notice that moment at the apex of the breath, when the incoming air encounters the outflowing air and the inhale becomes an exhale; when you have received the inspiration and you begin to expire.

To expire is to let go, succumb, and surrender. When you let go of the breath, let go with complete abandon. Get the tongue out of the way, open the throat, and let your breath flow freely through the throat—no pursed lips, no controlled release of the breath; complete abandon. Notice the sensation of expiring, letting go. When we hear another person exhale as in a sigh of relief, we know the feeling. That sensation of Ah! Make the sound. Fully surrender, as if the breath is being drawn from you. To truly let go of the breath is a feeling of trust, of faith that it is okay to release the breath. It is what we do when we feel safe. Feel the surrender in your own body as you let the breath be released and you feel the exhale of every cell in your body. We must let go in order to receive.

We speak of "letting go" as a concept. It is, indeed, a feeling. Imagine letting go. Let go of the grip in your hands. Turn your hands palms up and open. If you wish, grip your hands tightly first and then let go, to become conscious of the feeling of holding on, and then experience the full sensation of releasing. Do the same throughout the body. We hold on with many parts of our bodies, as if to control our experiences of being. Let go of the expression on your face and any effort to be seen in a certain way. We lift our brow as if to say, "I see what is going on here. I'm present and have an opinion." Let the brow release. Let the opinion go. Many of us hold a smile or grimace on our face. Let it go. Just be. Relax the tongue in the mouth and the eyes in their sockets. Like a puppy with its ears perked up, let your ears release down. Or like a dog that can make its hair stand on end, let the roots of your hair relax. Let go of the grip on your teeth. Exhale and release.

Some people purse their lips and blow out through their mouths. This is not what I'm suggesting. Restricting the flow of breath is restricting the relaxation response. Our efforts to control are consuming our energy. Give up control of the breath on the exhale, and let it be released with abandon. The inhale is like drawing back the string of a bow, and the exhale like letting an arrow fly.

Let go of the tension in your neck and shoulders. We speak of the sensation of carrying the weight of the world on our shoulders. Put the world down, and breathe into your shoulders. You may notice the gentle ebb and flow of the breath that gently moves and massages your shoulders as you breathe. If the shoulders are moving, check if there may also be the slightest motion of the breath through the arms. Imagine the motion of the breath flowing through the right shoulder and into the right arm, elbow, forearm, wrist, and onto the palm of the hand and the fingers; and through the left shoulder, flowing through the left arm, elbow, forearm, and wrist and into the palm of the left hand and the fingers. Feel the sensation of the air on the palms of your hands and the tips of your fingers, as if expecting the touch of a gentle breeze.

Let the breath fill the chest and feel the breath expanding and contracting the rib cage. We speak of having a heavy heart. Open your heart and let the heart be light. Breathe deeply and feel how the breath moves your chest and your ribs like the ebb and flow of waves at the beach, gently expanding and releasing through the body.

Position yourself so that the diaphragm can move freely and let the motion of the diaphragm massage your belly. We speak of the powerful sensations that arise in the belly, as in "That took some guts!" or "It was a gut- wrenching experience." Just now, breathe into the belly. Let the belly relax and let the breath flow down through the pelvis, as if breathing into your right hip and thigh, through the knee and down the calf, past the ankle, and into the sole of your right foot and your toes. Then imagine the breath flowing through the left hip and thigh and past the knee, shin, and ankle and into the sole of your left foot and toes, feeling the footprint on the soles of your feet.

When I suggest to children that they breathe into their toes, they show me their feet, literally expanding and contracting as if with each breath. I am certain that if the air were cold, we could see the breath coming off of their tiny toes. Try this just now: Clench your foot as if gripping a pencil with your toes and notice what happens to your belly and your breath. Clenching the toes contracts the abdominal muscles and interferes with the flow of the breath. Flexing the feet, freeing the toes, opens the root chakra, relaxes the belly, and allows the breath to move freely through the body.

In surrendering the breath, we make room for new inspiration. Notice the moment at the very bottom of the breath, that instant at the zenith of the exhale when the outflowing air begins to encounter the inflowing air and the exhale again begins to become an inhale. To *respire* is a constant cycle of receiving inspiration and letting go. Simply notice the experience as it ebbs and flows with each breath through your body. Notice the experience of being breathed, filling with creative energy and then expiring, surrendering, letting go with complete abandon, to receive again. Take five intentionally deep breaths, feeling the effects of the oxygen flowing into your brain. It can be dizzying as you breathe deeply, oxygenate the brain, and let go of the busy pattern of thinking in the head. Keep breathing.

As you breathe, your entire body breathes. As breath flows into the lungs, oxygen is absorbed through the lungs into the bloodstream. In the bloodstream, oxygen is carried to every living cell in the body. Each cell receives this oxygen, takes it in, metabolizes it, and uses this oxygen to create energy, and then exhales.

As you close your eyes and notice the experience of breathing, you may feel the sensation of the cells in your body themselves breathing and producing energy and the radiance and vibrancy of this energy emanating from your physical body.

We breathe not only through our nostrils and our mouth, but also through our skin. We take in oxygen through our skin and we release carbon dioxide through our skin. It is the scent of carbon dioxide released from our veins that attracts mosquitoes in the summertime. Feel the body breathing through every pore of your being. Witness the experience of breathing and being.

CHAPTER 9
The Senses

BODILY AWARENESS

The emotional brain-processes not only resemble the ordinary sensorial brain-processes, but in very truth are nothing but such processes variously combined...A purely disembodied human emotion is a nonentity.[56]

-William James
What is an Emotion (1884)

IN ADDITION TO DIRECTING YOUR focus on the breath, you may direct your point of focus toward other senses as well. Attend to the sounds around you, becoming conscious of the noises that you hear, as well as the effect of these sounds. Rather than focusing on that which is causing the noise, notice your own experience of *hearing*.

You may also notice the sensations of sight. Close your eyes when you finish this sentence and notice the light and dark on the inside of your eyelids, or the visions in your mind's eye, shifting your focus from that which you are observing to the experience of being an observer. Similarly, let your awareness shift to your sense of smell and taste. Even if there is no specific scent or aroma, notice what it is like to direct your awareness to the senses in your nose and your mouth. It is not about what you find when you look. The practice is to witness the experience, with a sense of curious awe. Even when the experience causes a reaction within you, sense the reaction. Notice the relation between the stimulus and then the response. The ability to self-regulate exists within that moment between the stimulus and the response. By attending to your reactions to the sensations of your experience, you will discover the moment of self-control

We've relinquished our control of self to conditioning. While conditioning provides a powerful resource in a life-or-death situation where an immediate unfiltered response may be best, conditioned responses such as the stress response of the sympathetic nervous system can overwhelm us when they become part of our everyday routine. Freedom from the conditioned response is found in practicing awareness of the sensate experience of the stimulus. Notice the sensation of sound, sight, smell, taste, and touch. Notice the experience of being in the flow. Let your awareness shift down into the other senses within your body. Notice the sensation of the air on your face and hands, and your clothing on your body.

There are many senses beyond the five that we are taught in school of sight, sound, smell, taste, and touch. Proprioception is the ability to sense one's orientation in space. It is truly the sense of gravity and our relation to this force. It is a sense of your relationship with the earth. Whether you experience it as a force that draws you toward the earth, or a force that presses you and the earth together, it is a feeling of connection. We often take the sense of gravity for granted, because it is ever-present. However, if the sensation of gravity were to suddenly shift, or even to disappear, you would certainly notice that something had changed. You may notice this when you take an elevator to the top of a skyscraper and step off suddenly. The sense of shift can affect your balance and you may feel heavier. Astronauts who go into outer space notice a shift in their proprioceptive experience. The sensation of gravity is indeed a sense of balance. It allows us to know which way is up, and which way is down. It orients us in space, giving us a sense of being grounded and connected with the earth. Because of the constancy of the presence of this sensation, we filter it out of our consciousness. And then we wonder why we feel disconnected or off-center. Any time that you wish to feel grounded, centered, or balanced, just direct your awareness to the sensation of gravity, and breathe.

You may imagine yourself resting at the base of a big tree, letting your energy join with the roots of the tree and extend deep down into the earth. Let your energy flow down into the earth, the way that the sap in the trees flows down into the roots. And breathe. Allow your body to rest in that sensation just now and feel the force that connects you to the earth. Allow the earth to hold you now.

The earth is truly the perfect mother. She is constantly there for us, holding us, allowing us to take her for granted, yet giving us the freedom to move as we choose. Rest in this sensation of embrace as you open your awareness to the feeling of gravity and succumb to the experience of being held. Any time that you are looking for a sense of being grounded or balanced, pause and allow your consciousness to open to the sensation of the force that connects you with the earth. When you feel the sensation of being held, it allows you to relax deeper into that embrace. The deeper you go, the more relaxed you become, and the more relaxed you become, the deeper you go. From these sensations of grounding and balance, other experiences can arise in your awareness, such as feelings of connectedness, safety, trust, and equanimity. And in that peace arises a sense of opening.

CHAPTER 10

The Mind: Dealing with Thoughts

THE VOICE WITHIN

YOU MAY NOTICE THAT THERE is often a little voice that speaks to us in a critical fashion. Whatever its nascent source, this voice sounds something like, "Oh I wish I would be like this…" (insert thinner, more organized, timely, or any type of "better" person). Or, "I've gotta stop…" (insert eating so much, smoking, chewing my nails, getting frustrated, or ruminating over unpleasant thoughts, etc.). This excessive activity in our brains is commonly referred to as the "monkey mind." I have heard a myriad of descriptions of what this brain activity feels like, including "the hum of a hive of bees," "Pop Rocks®," "the feeder-line on the bottom of CNN," "Post-it Notes® blowing all around." My friend Sierra Bender, author of the book on empowering women, *Goddess to the Core®*[57], refers to this voice as "The Itty Bitty Shitty Committee." Whatever you name your voice, know that with meditation practice, you can affect its attitude.

Upon settling into your meditation practice, most people have unsynchronized activity in various brain parts and, truly, throughout the body. The left temporal area may be emitting one frequency of energy while the frontal cortices are functioning at another, and the hind- brain may be emitting yet another frequency and amplitude of electromagnetic energy, and so on. It's a bit like an orchestra warming up before the symphony, as each instrument is doing its own thing in an unconcerted manner.

EEG studies of meditators show that as we settle into our practice, these brain-wave frequencies become synchronized, such that the entire brain becomes harmonized and all of the various brain parts ebb and flow in unison. With practice, the electromagnetic field of the entire body becomes harmonized, and the orchestration of the many bodily functions begins to play in unison, like a symphony. As the brain waves emanating from the various parts of the brain become more coherent, the quality of the experience shifts such that the phenomenon in its entirety is more magnificent than the sum of the individual instruments. The symphony takes on a nature of its own. When asked to report the nature of the little voice inside at this point, people who meditate report that they feel like they are who they want to be, and they want to be who they are!

SENSING THOUGHTS

The practice is to sit in a state of curious awareness of the experience of breathing and being. There is much to this. One of the first things that people notice when they tune in to what is going on in their experience of being is the multitude of thoughts that go through their head. The best approach to this busyness, and all other experiences that one may encounter in looking inward, is to allow it all to happen. Allow the mind to do whatever it is doing. And take note of what it is like. Become the observer of the experience that is occurring to your body, and yes, your head is part of your body. It is interesting to note that as you witness the process of thinking, with practice, things start to shift. The process is similar to running on a treadmill and then stepping off suddenly. If you try this, you may notice that when you step off of the treadmill, you still have a sensation of forward momentum. If you engage this sensation and start running forward again, the sensation will not necessarily go away.

However, if you are still and simply observe the sensation of forward momentum in your body, it will start to dissipate and eventually it will subside. The same is true of our "monkey mind" experience. Once we become aware of the sensation of momentous activity in our brains, rather than reacting by engaging in further thoughts, if we simply note the activity, and observe the experience, it too will eventually dissipate.

We are taught from an early age to use our intellectual capacity to process, analyze, calculate, and otherwise "think" our way through school and other complexities of modern life. We get the momentum of energy in our heads flowing at such a great speed that when we allow it to slow down, if we let go too quickly of our mental grasp, it can feel unusual, even "dizzying" or disorienting. It is helpful that our brains can function at such a fast and multidimensional capacity. If you drive a car, care for a family, go to school, or work at most jobs these days, you need to be able to think quickly, multitask, and process thoughts at great speed. Everything from the way that movies are programmed these days to move quickly from one scene and topic to another, to the way we multitask through numerous text messages, emails, and other electronic devices, reprograms our brains to be reactive and to shift our focus swiftly from one thing to another. We hardly notice that we've been running on this modern-day treadmill of executive thinking at a breakneck speed. We get unfamiliar with the sensation of stepping off of this treadmill of thought-provoking brain activity. We get out of the habit of slowing our cognitive processing and simply taking in the experience at hand. Yet we crave to let go.

As you reflect on the experience of thinking, you will notice that there is a sensation to this experience. When we think, we are able to detect where in our body the process of "thinking" is occurring. This may be so obvious that we take it entirely for granted. However, if you consider where you feel thinking occurring, we don't typically report the experience in our knees. We point to our head when we say we have had a thought. We know thoughts occur in our heads because we actually feel them there. When we experience thinking, we refer to the activity of the organ in our head called our brain, where we feel the sensation of thoughts occurring.

When "thoughts" distract you from your focus on the breath, simply take note of your sensations of thinking. Thoughts move through our head. As energy flows through your brain, you may sense your thoughts moving through your head. Note what you feel when a thought arises and makes its way through your brain. Thoughts don't just dwell in one place. There is a sense of flow with thinking. The same thought may come again and again, but there is an active momentum as it circles around for another pass.

Where does your thought arise, and what is its path as it flows through your head? Does it arrive on one side of your head and pass through to the other? Or does it arise from below and pass through the top, as in "A thought came up for me today." Or perhaps you feel thoughts arise in the center of your head and expand outwards. Do your thoughts move quickly and dart through your mind, or do they flow, hum, or dissipate? Or do they appear to jump around like a monkey in a tree—hence the reputation for "monkey mind"? Notice the sensation of thinking. Observe the energetic experience of thoughts as they move through your brain.

Note also the sensation of the space between the thoughts. Perhaps notice what it feels like as the breath flows into this space. And continue to breathe into this space. Then watch for the next thought to arise and, again, notice its qualities. Notice how the thoughts and the breath mingle. As you witness both the breath and your thoughts in your awareness, observe how their rhythms converge. Eventually you may notice a synchrony of the rhythms of breath, brain, and heart.

SOMATIC SENSING

But not even a Darwin has exhaustively enumerated all the bodily affections characteristic of any one of the standard emotions. More and more,

as physiology advances, we begin to discern how almost infinitely numer-
ous and subtle they must be.[58]

-William James
What is an Emotion (1884)

If thoughts are the experience of waves of electromagnetic energy moving through your head, sensations are the experience of external energy
waves making contact with your body, activating your sense organs, and
giving rise to an experience of this energetic flow as it passes into and
perhaps through you. At an early age, we learn about the five senses, including the senses of sound, sight, smell, taste, and touch. When sound
waves touch our eardrums, these physical waves impact the eardrum and
are thus transmitted through the eardrum and the cochlea to auditory
nerves, which send waves of electromagnetic energy flowing to the auditory cortex and other parts of the brain. We interpret this experience as
hearing a sound. It is known that people who are deaf are also capable
of experiencing the effects of sound, as sound waves can travel through
other parts of the body, being "heard" even through the soles of the feet.
Perhaps everyone can experience sound waves throughout their body;
however, the effects of hearing through the ears may distract people who
can "hear" from noticing these subtler physical sensations of sound waves.

Similarly, our eyes are uniquely equipped to respond to light waves
that impact our retina. Electromagnetic waves of energy in the visible
range impact the neural receptors in our eyes, causing an electrochemical
reaction, and thus sending electrical waves into the brain. Nerves in the
eye, such as the rods and cones, contain a light-sensitive chemical called
rhodopsin. When exposed to specific wavelengths of energy, rhodopsin
undergoes a chemical change. Typically purple in color, certain wavelengths of energy cause rhodopsin to become bleached of its color. In this
state, rhodopsin becomes a neurochemical activating the neurons in the

retina of the eye, triggering a flow of electrochemical reactions through the optic nerve and relaying this message to the visual processing cortex of the brain.

Interestingly, rhodopsin is found in other organisms as well. While it is an essential mechanism in the function of all visual processing (that is, if an animal has an eye, it has rhodopsin), it was also present in the earliest prehistoric one-celled organisms in the fossil record. Referred to as the "purple bacteria," by Carl Woese, who established this phylum in 1987, Proteobacteria contained rhodopsin within their cell.[59] These sea-dwelling creatures were sensitive to light, feeding at night and resting by day. During the daytime, the rhodopsin was bleached by light, causing the purple color to turn to white. The bacteria responded by burrowing under a layer of sand to protect themselves from the ionizing radiation of the sun. It is there in the fossil record that we find them, burrowed under the fossilized layers of sand. The ability to sense and respond to light waves is as primordial as the first inkling of life on this planet. It is this same mechanism of light-sensitivity that has been incorporated into the intricate mechanisms of our eyesight.

As you sense light, that "sensation" is literally the flow of an electro-chemical reaction in your eye and from your eyes to your brain. It is not that the bleaching of rhodopsin *causes* the sensation, like one domino in a series may cause another to fall. The bleaching of rhodopsin and the subsequent energy flow into and through the brain actually *is* the experience of light. Through learning and conditioning in childhood, we have come to associate the sensation of the flow of energy with the specific patterns of light that we claim to see and with the words that we use to describe these patterns. This sensation of light becomes integrated with other perceptions and develops into a more complex pattern of stimulus, and conditioned response. For example, when we look into a starry night, we may have learned the names of the constellations and planets that we see. Or when we look at a friend, we recognize "friend" along with all of the other

associated emotional responses that we have learned through conditioning. But these names are not the *experience* of seeing the constellations
or our friend. That experience is a much richer dimension of the state of
being. The unique quality of being alive is the sensation of the flow of
energy through our bodies, as our bodies are impacted by waves of energy
from the surrounding environment, and in reaction, as the neurons in our
sense organs communicate with neurons in our brains, radiating energy
fields through and around us. That is the sense of *The Flow*.

Feelings: The Sensate Basis of Our Emotions

If we wish to conquer undesirable emotional tendencies in ourselves, we must assiduously, and in the first instance cold-bloodedly go through the outward motions of those contrary dispositions we prefer to cultivate.[60]

-William James,
What is an Emotion (1884)

When asked how we *feel*, one can answer from a number of perspectives. One might simply say "Fine," with no real reflection on the feelings within, simply a gratuitous response to a gratuitous question. Or, we could respond on an emotional level and say, "I feel hungry," "I feel happy," "I feel stressed-out," "I'm about to collapse," or "I feel wonderful." These statements of emotional condition are labels that we put on an actual somatic experience. We learn from an early age to label this interoceptive experience so that we can quickly communicate it, and so that others can quickly relate or empathize with us.

We can be even more specific about these sensations as we learn to be conscious of the somatic sensing of emotions—indeed, our *feelings*. For example, you might note, "I feel the sensation of relaxing, opening, and becoming lighter." We can become aware that what we refer to as feelings actually arise from specific sensations in the body, shifting senses of the flow within. We can feel palpitations in our hearts, or wrenching in our guts. We can feel shortness of breath, or spasms in our backs. We can even feel and learn to be conscious of our hearts opening and expanding.

Emotions like "love," "guilt," "sorrow," or "happiness" are labels that we apply to actual physical sensations. When you pause to reflect in a meditative state, paying attention to interoceptive sensations, you may gradually become more conscious of these internal experiences. When we report an emotional state, such as sad or happy, sleepy, hungry, or love, we are making a quick scan of our physical sensations and then instantaneously applying labels to these sensations. Meditation is a time to reflect on the very basic sensations of shifting energies in the body. Interpretation of bodily sensations of energetic shifts happens so spontaneously that we may not notice the connection. Indeed, this frequently unnoticed relationship between bodily sensation and emotion may define the concept of "subconsciousness." With practiced awareness, you can reconnect the mind and body experience. As you become aware, or conscious, of the physical experience in your body that you are interpreting as a mood state, you are literally expanding your consciousness.

Emotional labels are learned and communicated to us as we learn language in infancy and childhood. Different people may interpret sensations differently, applying emotional labels differently than others. These spontaneous interpretations of our physical experience become second nature to us. We rarely slow down the process enough to interpret the initial bodily sensations giving rise to our emotions. These physical body sensations remain "subconscious," literally below the consciousness of the brain. But they are not without effect. They are the substance of what we call our emotions. The physical sensations of shifting energy that arise from your body are indeed your *feelings.*

People have different levels of interoceptive sensitivity; we are all differently gifted. We take music lessons to learn to play an instrument. We take art lessons to learn to portray visual images. By learning to meditate you will cultivate your interoceptive awareness of somatic experiences, the foundation of emotional intelligence. All evidence suggests that enhanced awareness of interoceptive experiences improves the capacity for self-regulation and self-control. The capacity for self-regulation and self-control are the tools for developing social and emotional intelligence.

When you reflect on your internal experience, be aware of the various somatic experiences, and the tendency to label these sensations, as well as the associated thoughts that accompany your feelings. I identify three levels for defining experience. The most common in our culture is The Story. Whenever I hear someone say, "I feel this way *because…*", I know that I am about to hear The Story. Your story is a poetic perspective on what is happening to you, trying to connect reason with how you actually feel. Discussing *why* you may feel a certain way externalizes the locus of control and does not provide the same tools for personal growth as an interoceptive perspective of your experience. Working in the realm of The Story affords you little benefit if you want to change the way that you feel.

The second level for defining experience is The Emotion. Remember, emotions are just labels for somatic experiences of energy states within the body. They are not entities that we can put on a shelf or hand to someone else. The ephemeral nature of the concepts we refer to as emotions and mood states make it so much harder to control one's experience from this perspective. As no more than a concept, moods and emotions have no tangible nature. Concepts are subject to interpretation, and they are not within our control the way that we can control a physical part of our body. We falsely identify control of feelings to outside sources, as in "You hurt my feelings," or "He stresses me out."

There is a foundation to our emotions, which is the third level for defining experience — The Sensation. Our sensations are the somatic experience or feeling of energy shifting that arises within the body, such as the heart closing or opening, sinking or uplifting. Once you can connect your consciousness with feelings or sensations, energetic shifts within the body, then you can begin to learn to coordinate and control these experiences. By defining these three perspectives of our experience of being, *story, emotions, and sensations,* we discover a way to control the experience of being and to create the experiences of our choosing. In all situations, our experience is derived from a physical sensation in our body.

You can build a muscle by exercising it, but a prerequisite to any muscle building is the creation of nerve networks from the brain to the muscle to control the actions of that muscle. By developing these nerve networks from brain to muscle, we develop what we refer to as coordination—the capacity to self-regulate with intention. This same type of coordination applies to all of the activities of the body. When we practice awareness of the activity, we cultivate coordination and the capacity for self-regulation. What would you like to learn to control? What sensate experience would you like to cultivate within you? The sensation of your heart expanding: Notice when you feel it and all the details of the heart's energy filling your chest and radiating from you. The sensation of peace in your mind, settling over your entire body: Notice what it feels like as peace settles over you just now. A calm sensation of groundedness, balance, and connection with the earth: Check on your experience just now. These are the sensations of waves of energy moving through your body. In the core of your consciousness of this energy, you hold the capacity for self-regulation and self-control.

OTHER SENSES

Our proprioceptive sense of gravity as a force that connects us with the earth is not the only sense of gravity that affects us. We are well aware of the concept of the effect of the moon's gravitational pull on our human behavior. The words loony and lunatic, referring to human behavior during a full moon, come from the Latin word for moon, lune. The gravitational pull of the moon is powerful enough to drag the oceans back and forth across the face of the earth, giving rise to the shifting tides. The subtle sense of shift in the force of the moon's gravity during its twenty-eight-day cycle is enough to control the cyclic changes in reproductive hormones in humans and many other species. Many sea-dwelling creatures that find their homes along the tidal coastline also find their reproductive behavior regulated by the gravity of the moon. In studies designed to determine whether animals are sensing the absence/presence of the tide, or actually the gravity of the moon, researchers found that even in the absence of the flow of water, animals are sensing the force of the moon's gravity.

Other cycles of the universe also influence our behavior and sense of well-being. Many of our hormone levels are interestingly tied to these galactic shifts. The obvious daily cycle of the earth in relation to the sun, as the earth spins on its axis, creates the cycle of night and day. This cycle conspicuously affects our wakefulness and sleepiness as our cortisol levels rise and fall in the twenty-four-hour period. Our cortisol levels naturally subside during the early evening, inviting us to be sleepy at night and begin to rise in the pre-dawn hour, awakening us, sometimes "with the birds."

Our relationship with the sun is also sensitive to annual cycles, as the earth cycles through the galaxy, tilting toward the sun in the northern summers, and away from the sun in the northern winters. As with other animals, the annual cycle of the relation of earth and sun also affects our hormones, reproductive cycles, growth, and metabolism. We sense these shifts in the flow of the universe around us. Whether we do so consciously or not, we can tell that our bodies are affected by the physiological shifts that occur. We may tune out these experiences, filtering them as we do with white noise. Yet we long for the sense of flow that connects us with the rhythms of the universe.

Seasonal Affective Disorder is a diagnosis given to a seasonal sense of feeling low that besets at the beginning of winter. It occurs at a time when our metabolism slows, our appetite shifts, and other hormonal changes occur. To me, it is a natural phenomenon, and when I embrace it, I stay in the flow. When the season shifts at the end of autumn, there are many other signs of energy levels dropping. The trees drop their leaves, and the sap flows down into the tree's roots. Animals that can leave do so, and those that stay prepare for hibernation or other lower levels of energy. The world rests around us. And yet I sense this as a time when the human community is not always in alignment with the rest of the environment. We stick to our regular routine at work; kids have exams and schoolwork. We have celebrations of holidays and all of the preparatory activity that goes with that. Stress levels are high. We are doing anything but hibernating. When we feel the powerful sense of surrendering to the environmental energy around us, a sense of fatigue or exhaustion, we call it a disorder. Labeling ourselves with a diagnosed disorder surely must make us feel even worse. The disorder may simply be resisting the urge to slow down. The disorder is not in wanting to curl up in a cozy bed and rest, but in maintaining the hectic schedules and activities in our lives that go against the natural flow of energy at this time of year. The good news is that we are humans; we don't need to hibernate to get synchronized with the cycles of nature. By normalizing the experience of slowing down in the winter and permitting yourself some time to completely surrender and succumb to the urge to rest, you will find that you are soon replenished and rejuvenated and that you can stay in the flow through the year. Meditating during times of shifting seasons can help to smooth the transitions, regulating moods as well as physical and emotional well-being.

As you relax into your meditation, you may become more sensitive to and aligned with these cycles and the natural sense of flow. When you feel your energy levels coming down, so be it. Simply observe. Other times you will feel your energy levels rising. Bear witness to that as well. As you practice your meditation and your consciousness opens, remember, it is not about what you find in your consciousness, it is that you look. By bearing witness in that curious state of awareness, you are practicing meditation. The uninhibited practice of awareness is what frees the innate healing capacities of the physical body. See what your exploration reveals to you.

PART 3

Heart Sensing

CHAPTER 11

Momentum

Do you remember when you were a child, the sensation of spinning around and around in a circle? I would do it until I dropped to the ground on my back and then I'd watch the world continue spinning, while I'd lie there perfectly still. The world was not really spinning (well it was, but not perceptibly so), but the momentum of my earlier movement persisted in my body and my mind. As I'd lie perfectly still, the sensation of momentum from my earlier movement gradually faded, until the whole world began to feel still again.

Nowadays I don't twirl as much, but I do like to sail. I notice a similar phenomenon after sailing. There is a sense of the movement of the boat even after I get off of the boat. The rhythm of our lives gains a momentum, and the sensation of that momentum persists even after the force that caused it is gone.

Where I feel the momentum most nowadays is the momentum of what impacts my mind. We live in a culture of multitasking and high-speed thinking. Driving requires that we pay attention to a multitude of factors at the same time. We may be good at it, but it creates a momentum. I pick up my phone to make a call, and there are a dozen text messages and emails blinking at me. The activities of modern life create a momentum in our minds that we sense as mental activity. This momentum affects the senses in our body and can begin to affect our health. The Thalamic Gates close and the upper spheres of our conscious brain seem to be bouncing around like the ball in a pinball machine. We spend less and less time attending to the physical sensations arising from the body, essentially ignoring the part of the self that extends from the mouth down.

The momentum of your thoughts may continue into the stillness when you sit to meditate. The momentum of the mind becomes familiar. It even becomes a habit. When at first we begin to downshift and let the momentum of the mind unwind, it may feel unfamiliar, even strange.

When we shut down the Thalamic Gates, sensing into the body is forgotten. Experiencing the sensations of our body is delegated to the subconscious realms. As we lose conscious awareness of the physical sensations of experience, we lose control of these realms, affecting our physical health and overall well-being. The capacity to self-regulate the finely tuned biochemical and physiological balance of the bodily systems is ignored and can get off balance. This is particularly true when things change, such as life situations, relationships, job environments, living environments, even the changing of the seasons. Our hormones are closely tied to the rhythms of the seasons and other cycles in our lives. So we become resistant to change, because we sense the imbalance when things change. We cling to the familiar however uncomfortable it may be, longing to let go. Yet things do change. The seasons cycle; the moon cycles; days and nights come and go. Yet we resist.

Energy has a momentum. Newton's First Law of Motion says that every object in motion tends to remain in that state of motion, unless an external force is applied to it.[61] A body in motion tends to stay in motion until it encounters another force. During meditation, the waves of momentum that we create with hectic activities of daily living merge with the force of the natural rhythms around us. We get back in the flow.

We do not live in a vacuum or a still universe. Our measure of days, months, and years is evidence that we experience cycles, shifting momentums. Our measure of time indicates that our lives synchronize with the sense of time, the sense of flow. We live in a universe of motion. The natural state is a sense of flow. When we rebalance through meditation, we align with the momentum of the energies around us and we enter this realm of flow. Getting back in the flow is about using mindfulness to regain consciousness of being. Being in the flow means allowing the momentum of the mind its natural tendency to synchronize with the flow, so that the Thalamic Gates can open, the consciousness can expand, and the fullness of the experience of being can arise. Breathe, and know, it is safe to let go.

CHAPTER 12

Perspectives on Being: Creating Sensate Awareness

The Relationship Between Thoughts, Feelings, and Emotions

You may notice that when you begin your meditation practice, the accumulated energetic momentum of using the brain for multitasking and executive thinking is predominantly present in your consciousness. In essence, it feels like you are thinking. Thoughts arise as bursts of electromagnetic fields flowing through your head. And they will continue until the momentum has a chance to subside.

The question, "What do you think?" is a very different question and garners a different response from the question, "How do you feel?" For example, if I was asked what I *think* about global warming, I might go on and on about why it is occurring, what we can do about it, how it is affecting us, and how it will continue to affect us. However, if asked how I *feel* about global warming, I might simply respond that I feel a bit uneasy about it.

Thinking is a phenomenon that we use our heads to do. It is an analytical process in which we use our brains to generate energetic patterns that we experience as thoughts, ideas, opinions, judgments, concerns, plans—like our to-do list or memories. While we experience these thoughts as an experiential phenomenon, thoughts are simply electromagnetic waves of energy flowing through our brains. Thoughts are related to changes in the vibrational frequencies and electromagnetic output of the cells of our brains.

106

In my research using electroencephalography, I measured the flow of electromagnetic waves of energy through the brain. In a subject who is awake, the flow shifts quickly, and it is qualitatively different in different parts of the brain. Waves of energy flow through each area of the brain as thoughts are processed. Various parts of the brain seemingly "talk" to each other through this energetic flow.

In a subject who is in deep, slow-wave sleep, the electromagnetic fields of the brain flow in unison, in long, slow rhythmic waves of electrical and magnetic activity. There is coherence between activities in different regions of the brain.

When you stop the twirling of a busy mind, there may be some residual momentum. Thoughts may continue to float through the brain. When you meditate, rather than engaging these thoughts, simply observe them and their gradually shifting momentum, just as you might observe the sense of physical momentum from movement. If you twirled, stopped, sensed the momentum, and then instead of stopping and observing, engaged that sense of movement by continuing to twirl, the twirling would continue, unending. Instead, in meditation simply permit the sensation of mental momentum to be there and observe it. It will dissipate. Breathe and observe the sense of flow of thoughts merging with the flow of the breath as you meditate. You will eventually find yourself observing the space between the thoughts and the qualities of this space itself. It is like observing the sky and watching clouds clear. As you focus on that single remaining cloud floating by on a breeze, even that cloud evaporates in the blueness of the sky, and you are left observing the sky itself.

THE STORY, EMOTIONS OR ENERGY

Modern civilization has become divorced from the transcendent realm, which in former ages was consciously integrated into daily life. The modern world fails to understand the meaning of the word transcendent as well as the meaning of the word intellect. In the traditional usage—which corresponds to the Sanskrit word for mind, buddhi—intellect means the perception of transcendent realities, the faculty that can perceive the activity of the higher worlds... We can see here that the intellect is a faculty for perceiving, directly, our relationship with higher realities rather than something someone acquires through study and schooling.[62]

-René Guénon
The Crisis of the Modern World (1942)

As we regain a fuller sense of the experiences of being, there are different perspectives from which we can describe the experiences that emerge. I explain to my students that there are three options (see Figure 2).

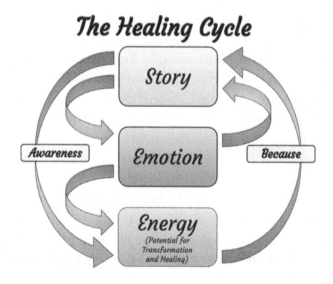

FIGURE 2. Perspectives on experience can include the story, the emotion, and/or the energy. "Because..." is often a prelude to someone telling a story about themselves. Awareness allows us to perceive the emotions that underlie our story and the energetic state that is the basis for our emotions and stories. It is through our awareness of our energetic state that we find the potential for change, transformation, and healing, as we discover the ability to shift and change our energetic state.

1. *The Story.* We can talk about the story of our lives, discussing who did what, when, and why. Whenever I hear the word "because" I know we are working from the perspective of the story. For example, "I only said that to him because of what he said to me." I often observe my students becoming breathless as they recount these stories, holding their breath and their tension as they talk.

2. *Emotions.* We can talk about the emotions that we use to label our experiences. This often occurs within the context of recounting the story. For example, "I became upset when he did that"; or "I get anxious when she always does that to me." If I probe deeper about feelings, the reply might be, "Well, it makes me feel nervous or depressed." We can talk about emotions, but again, emotions are just labels that we apply to somatic sensations. This is an okay place to start, but labeling emotion is only the first step in shifting the experience of being. At least by labeling an emotion, we can recognize that a personal experiential phenomenon is occurring.

3. *Energy.* We can explore the actual sensate basis of the experiential phenomenon. The theme of this experiential process is recognized in the practices of somatic sensing, body scanning, and other ways of employing interoceptive awareness. In exploring the experiential nature of our existence, we cultivate the ability to describe the actual energetic state of our body, and any shifts that are occurring in this sensation. Once we discover the underlying physical nature of our experience, and the shifting sensations of energy moving, we learn how to change this energetic state and in so doing change our experience. By changing the underlying energetic state of our physical being, we change what we perceive as our emotions and, correspondingly, our story.

In mindfulness practices, we bring the realm of the subconscious, ultimately the full potential of the human organism's experience, into the conscious. By breathing deeply and creating a sense of safety, we open the Thalamic Gates, letting awareness in. Pow! That makes a difference in people's lives!

This process can be done gradually, which is recommended for people who have suffered trauma or extreme stress. Or it can happen suddenly, as with people who experience a Kundalini Awakening, in which practitioners report a sudden spiritual emergence. Yogis describe the phenomenon of the Kundalini Awakening as the experience of all of the seven major chakras in the body, from the base of the spine to the top of the head, opening suddenly and the consciousness experiencing a sudden expansion (the opening of the Thalamic Gates).

Remember, stress and trauma are associated with closing of the Thalamic Gates, narrowing of focus and decreased somatic awareness, delegating more of our function to the realm of the subconscious. This lower baseline level of consciousness creates the potential for an even more dramatic change as the consciousness expands. Since our culture is not familiar with such a sudden awakening, even people who have not been traumatized may retreat from the experience of gradually increasing somatic awareness, much less what is called a Kundalini Awakening experience, if they are not guided carefully to understand what is happening to them. The practice must be grounded in the confidence that the experience is safe. The sense of safety and the ability to use the breath to create this sense of safety must be thoroughly grounded in a foundation of trust, whether trust in teacher, trust in self, or trust in God. Trust, faith, and belief create a sense of safety and ease. These are the emotional labels that we put on the sensation we experience as our hearts and our minds open.

The nature of expanding awareness is by definition taking us into an experiential realm that is unfamiliar and unique. If you haven't been aware of a sensory experience, and now you are, it can feel unusual or weird. The description of this type of experience can be similar to what mental health providers may interpret as a psychotic break, so people can become afraid when these experiences are reported. Fear erodes the primary foundation of the sense of safety. Using the breath as a tool to maintain a sense of safety and groundedness is key to gradually unlocking the gates and pacing the opening of the subconscious. By focusing on the breath, you can maintain the sense of connection with the flow. The breath becomes a tool for maintaining a mindful sense of relaxation and ease as the consciousness expands.

I once had a student who came to me wishing to learn to meditate. She said that she had been practicing on her own, but that she was doing something wrong and it was not working for her. She said that she was also diagnosed with a mental health condition and was being medicated by her psychiatrist. As we began the practice, she quickly reported experiencing a sense of light; a bright white light seemed to be emerging throughout her being so she wanted to stop. I invited her to keep breathing and to let the light continue to emerge, that it was safe to experience this sense of light. She stopped abruptly, opened her eyes, and explained to me that she had reported this sense of light while meditating to her husband. He found this experience too weird and had insisted on taking her to a psychiatrist to have her evaluated. When she explained the experience to her psychiatrist, she was given a prescription for antipsychotic medication. Her psychiatrist was now medicating her to prevent her from experiencing this sensation of light. She had no other psychotic or neurotic symptoms. She was being treated with antipsychotic medications because she had reported a sense of light to her husband and psychiatrist. She was not supposed to experience this sense of light. That is why she came to me, she explained, to learn to meditate properly, without this weird sensation of light.

Having taught meditation for decades and having studied meditation with groups of people for even longer, I have witnessed many people report this sense of light as a result of meditating. I have also seen the longing of fellow classmates to experience this proverbial sense of the Light. (It can be awesome.) This is the light reported in biblical accounts of "Being in the Light." This is the light that lights the pathway for those who claim to "walk in the Light." This is the light that brings us out of the darkness of fear and pain. It is the light of an expanding consciousness. A sense of light is safe. It may or may not happen when you meditate. If it does happen to you, explore it. Breathe deeply and continue. It is not about what you find while you practice, but simply that you look, from a curious state of awareness. The primary foundation of this process is being mindful of a sense of safety and relaxation.

I have had my own experience of coming to the edge of the Great Abyss. Beyond the edge appeared to be darkness and doom. I took a gentle breath, and in my imagination, I turned my back to the abyss and let my-self fall backward into it. As I released into the fall, I yielded to the momentum that had been building up behind me, ready to push me forward with the flow. By clinging to my fears, I had become accustomed to the struggle of resistance. It was all just a physical sensation inside my body. When I let my body feel the sensation of surrender, like the surrender when we let go after we have been holding our breath, the sudden release allowed the momentum to propel me forward into the flow. Like a gasp of relief, I felt a sensation of a powerful beam of light emanate from deep in the abyss and lift me up into the light above, an amazing and uplifting experience. Now, rather than turning from them, I seek the edge of my fears. Once there, I breathe deeply and release myself into them.

Your fears will be different, they will be personal, and they will be familiar. How you release is your choice. Other experiences may also arise, of all different sorts. Resistance comes in many forms. So does the release. Remember that you are simply sitting in your comfortable meditation space, exploring the potential of the expanding consciousness. Pace yourself. We choose what we choose to hold on to, and we choose what we choose to let go of. As with life, some experiences are uncomfortable and some are comfortable. Simply explore the shifting momentum of energetic flow in the body and breathe. It is not about what you find in that curious state of awareness, but that you look.

You will become familiar with the process of encountering your resistance, exploring it, breathing at its edge, and then noticing as resistance dissolves into flow. In the stillness of meditation, we are exploring the sensations that arise in our body, and release from our minds. It is this same process that happens on the yoga mat or in qigong. We find the physical resistance where our mind is holding tension in the body, and then we find that place in the mind that gives the body permission to let go. We breathe at the edge of this resistance, playing there while our brains reconnect with the physical body, remembering how to coordinate it so that we can choose whether to hold on or to let go. As these neural pathways of energy are reopened, we feel more vibrant and more alive. With our emotional and physical coordination and flexibility we become radiant, powerful, and in the flow. Once you are familiar with the process it becomes easier. It is a continual process. We are never done. Enjoy the ride. The hills and the valleys are all there to remind us that we are alive.

THE MOMENT

The moment is that period of time during which your consciousness is directed at the momentum. The moment is when you are conscious of being in the flow. All around us, within us, and emanating from us are flows of energy. We know that light is waves of energy that emanate from the sun. Light is reflected and absorbed, blocked, captured, and released. We picture it as a single wave, the way we see a wavy line on a page. But light fills a room because it is everywhere in a room. In the same way, sound fills a room because it is everywhere in a room. Sound is the vibration of space. Sound does not just make a beeline from its source to our ear. It explodes from its source in all directions and dimensions, warping space and creating a percussion that is at least four-dimensional in nature. This percussion that we call sound hits our ears and is transmitted to our brains through electrical impulses, resulting in what we call hearing. By altering our state of flow, hearing can affect our mood and also our physical state of being.

Space is full of vibrational energies. Vibrations are not just interwoven; they are the sum and substance of the space in which we exist. When physicists explore down into the heart of matter and the very atoms that compose matter, there is nothing more than a flow of vibrating energy and light. When we check in on the energetic state of our being and our experience of the environment around us, when we direct our consciousness at the fullness of our experience of being, our consciousness responds by attuning us with this flow. Then we are in the flow.

We can alter our consciousness to focus more selectively, narrowing our range of sensitivity and increasing our intensity of focus on one point. You may have done this when listening to a full band or orchestra. With effort you may direct your focus on a single instrument, perhaps hearing only the violin, listening to the sound that it makes, while the other instruments play in the background. Alternatively, you may let go of your focus and simply bask in the experience of the entire orchestra, receiving the entirety of the symphonic experience as it flows through you. In this case, you have let your consciousness take a step back and simply be a witness to the experience of the symphony of waves of sound energy. You are in the flow.

You may begin your meditation practice single-pointedly, focused on one thing such as your breath or other sensate experience. Eventually, let your consciousness take a step back. Become the witness to the entirety of your experience. Experience the fullness of all of the sensate qualities of being. Let your consciousness open to the entire symphony of life.

What we know or experience is only that which impacts our physical state. We only hear those vibrations of space that impact our eardrums. We only see the light that impacts our retina. We only taste that which touches our tongue or smell that which touches our nostrils. And we only feel the touch that contacts our skin. What we sense is only that which actually impacts us physically. Our sense organs are simply refined structures for detecting specific vibrational energies that we encounter in space.

The ability to sense our environment is inherent in our survival. Our senses serve as a guide, allowing us to move toward food or other life-supporting resource and away from danger. As we move toward that which feels good and nourishes us, it supports our survival. As we move away from that which supports our survival, it feels bad. Similarly, we get an uneasy feeling as we move toward that which threatens us. It feels bad. Yet it feels like a relief to move away from danger.

We move away from pain and toward pleasure—not hedonic pleasure, but pleasure that serves both self and others. By being in the flow and directing your consciousness to the entirety of the energetic momentum impacting you, you can respond and direct your energies for moving you toward your purpose, toward that which feels good and right. This is the sense of being in the flow and using the sense of flow to find and fulfill your life's purpose.

Self-Awareness and Self-Regulation: Consciousness of Self Leads to Capacity for Self-Control

As humans, we perceive feelings from our bodies that relate our state of well-being, our energy and stress levels, our mood and disposition. How do we have these feelings? What neural processes do they represent? Recent functional anatomical work has detailed an afferent neural system in primates and in humans that represents all aspects of the physiological condition of the physical body. This system constitutes a representation of "the material me," and might provide a foundation for subjective feelings, emotion and self-awareness.[63]

-A. D. (Bud) Craig
Nature Reviews Neuroscience (2002)

...endogenous homeostatic control mechanisms modulate the integration of afferent activity that produces the feelings from the body, which underscores the crucial dependence of subjective well-being on the physiological health of the body. The emerging evidence from imaging studies that

volitional cortical control in humans can directly modify homeostatic integration and the substrate of the feeling self signifies the fundamental role of this interoceptive system in human consciousness.[64]

-A. D. (Bud) Craig
Trends in Cognitive Sciences (2003)

I once participated in a talk to a group of physicians in a hospital about the use of meditation as a form of therapy that can affect the brain. Scientist Andrea Caria and colleagues at the Institute of Medical Psychology and Behavioral Neurobiology in Germany had found that subjects receiving immediate feedback from fMRI about what was going on in their brains could learn very quickly to activate a specific part of the brain known as the anterior insular cortex or AIC.[65] The AIC is a very small portion of the brain, which plays a role in regulating consciousness, interoceptive awareness, and emotion, as well as homeostasis and the immune system. A physician in the audience was incredulous at the suggestion that we could actually learn to intentionally activate specific areas of the brain. How could someone learn to activate such a specific portion of the brain?

Tell me this. Hold up your right hand and wiggle your little pinky finger. How is it that you can make your pinky finger wiggle? You intend it to happen, and it does. Yes, nerve fibers fire and send messages along axons that synapse on muscles and muscles contract and the joints of the finger move. In the case of the AIC, nerve fibers fire and send messages along axons that synapse on receptors of the AIC, and the AIC becomes activated. In this way, we can intend experiences. We can activate memories; intend sensations of empathy or compassion; hone our senses; and with practice cultivate an enhanced sense of self-awareness.

When a person becomes aware of their AIC through the visual aid of fMRI brain imaging, they can quickly learn to self-regulate and control activation of this portion of the brain. With awareness comes the capacity for self-regulation and self-control. Though we don't always have an MRI machine to provide neurofeedback on our brains, meditation is the process of cultivating volitional control through interoceptive awareness. The various regions of the brain are responsible for specific functions of our body and the interoceptive experiences of being that we call feelings and emotions. As we allow our focus to explore within, we begin to find these somatic experiences and the functions that they regulate. Though we are not *seeing* activation of the AIC, we may be *feeling* it. Our awareness is our own feedback machine. Interoceptive awareness is the source of discovery of control of our brains, our experience of being and of ourselves.

THE BUILDING BLOCKS OF CONSCIOUSNESS

The nervous system of every living thing is but a bundle of predispositions to react in particular ways upon the contact of particular features of the environment.[66]

-William James
What is an Emotion (1884)

Consciousness is mainly attributed in our culture to the function of our central nervous system, or more specifically, our brains. A blow to the head or an anesthesia that works on our brains can cause us to "lose consciousness." The basic cellular unit of the nervous system, including the brain and the peripheral nervous system, is called the neuron. Neurons are the cellular units that allow for the sense of flow and communion between self and environment that we call sensation and feeling. Neurons are also responsible for processing information through the brain, decision making, contemplation, memory and thinking of all sorts, as well as propagation of reactive information from the brain out to our muscles and organs for action.

Neurons both receive and send information. Neurons are receptive to electromagnetic shifts and are capable of activating other cells via both electrical and chemical mechanisms. Neurons in the afferent pathways are receiving information, typically from some external source of energetic field, and propagating this information toward the brain. Neurons in the efferent pathways are part of information transmission from the brain to other parts of the body.

Neurons that synapse on other neurons appear to be transmitting information in the form of electrochemical reactions along neuronal tracts. Neurons that synapse on muscles are either activating or inhibiting action at these muscles; or they may be receiving information from the muscle (is it contracted, relaxed, or somewhere in between). Neurons that synapse at organs are also either transmitting guidance to the organ or receiving information from the organ.

From the perspective of our thoughts, the sensation that arises in our brain gives rise to the sensation of thinking. Studies of the active brain reveal that the sensation of energy flow through the brain is associated with specific electrochemical actions within our brain. Shifts occur in the neurochemistry of our brains as we think. Neurons fire in our brains as electrically charged ions such as sodium (Na+) and chloride (Cl-) move in and out of our cells, creating electromagnetic fields. These electromagnetic fields flow through different parts of our brains as we process different types of thoughts. We measure this energy as it flows through our heads using EEG and MRI. Energy can be observed flowing as electrical current along nerve fibers or as hot spots of electromagnetic resonance within specific brain regions. Energetic flow in the brain can channel along specific nerve tracts, or it can spread globally through parts of the brain. Energetic excitation of neuron cells is contagious. This global spreading of electrical excitation is the problem detected with seizures. Seizures typically have a focal point, and once that focal point is stimulated, electrical excitation generated from this focal point spreads throughout the brain or a region of the brain. As a wave of energy sweeps the brain, it creates havoc with our thoughts and loss of consciousness and all the other functions of self-regulation conducted by the brain. Alternatively, normal function weaves energetic flow along well-worn pathways through the brain. With EEG, we can detect shifting patterns of electrical current flowing through the brain the way that a murmuration of birds flow together, shape-shifting their way through the sky.

Just as the experience of electromagnetic waves moving through the head gives rise to the sensation of thoughts and the experience of thinking, the flow of energy moves beyond our brains and into the peripheral nervous system and the rest of the body. What we experience are these waves of electrical and magnetic current flowing through our nervous system, as well as through the muscles, organs, and indeed every living cell in our body. Waves of electromagnetic fields flowing through the body give rise to somatic sensations. As we practice interoceptive awareness of these somatic sensations, we begin to expand our consciousness and our capacity to heal.

The Energetics of Sensation

The human brain is a biological organ. On one hand it is soft, flexible and adaptive, but on the other hand is relatively stable and coherent with well developed intelligence. In order to retain intelligent thinking in a soft and adaptive organ there needs to be a constant, globally available, synchronization system that continuously stabilizes the brain. Rapid intelligence and reactions requires an electromagnetic signalling system, supported by a biochemical system. The Schumann Resonance signal provides a brain frequency range matching electromagnetic signal, providing the synchronization needed for intelligence.[67]

-Neil J. Cherry
Medical Hypotheses (2003)

As a neuroscientist studying exercise physiology, I found it interesting to note that muscle cells are similar to brain cells in that they regulate their function through the use of flow of charged ionic particles such as sodium (Na+), calcium (Ca+), magnesium (Mg+), and chloride (Cl-). Even a single-celled organism both senses and moves with that single cell, evidence that muscle cells and brain cells have a common origin. Perhaps these cells have more in common in the way that they function than we realize. Each cell in our body is sensitive and in some way responsive to the environment around it. Our cells are constantly sending and receiving messages from each other, communicating to enhance our collective well-being.

Neurons are sensitive to input which may serve to stimulate or "excite" the cell to action, causing it to propagate electrochemical messages on to the next neuron in the neuronal sequence. Many neurotransmitters, and drugs which may simulate these neurochemicals, function to excite the cell—as agonists activating specific neurons. Amphetamine drugs and the neurotransmitters that they simulate, such as dopamine and serotonin, are examples of excitatory chemicals. Other input may serve to inhibit activation of neurons or clusters of nerve cells. Drugs that act as antagonists block the action potential of nerve cells. Naloxone is a well-known drug that acts as an antagonist, blocking the action of excitatory neurotransmitters and the drugs that act on them, such as endogenous endorphins and exogenous heroin and morphine.

When a neural circuit is activated, neurons transmit a sequence of electrochemical events that flow through the brain like the flow of a series of dominoes, activating one cell or cluster of cells after another. This flow of electrochemical reactions can permeate the whole body via neural and muscle cell reactions. Though medical science and practice have focused primarily on the chemical dimension of these pathways for transmission of consciousness, the electrophysical properties of cellular communication are also critical to understanding the practice and experience of mindfulness.

Human beings are bioelectrical systems. Our hearts, brains, and other body systems are regulated by internal bioelectrical signals. Electroencephalographic study of the brain shows that nerve cells, just like all other cells in our bodies, are sensitive to and responsive to subtle shifts in electrical and magnetic fields. The application of a tiny electrical pulse is sufficient to activate the firing of our cells. Cells communicate with each other using electrical impulses. Those + and – charges carried by chemical ions such as sodium and chloride are the source of the electrical current that flows through our bodies.

Modern medical devices measure this flow of electromagnetic waves using diagnostic imaging techniques such as EEG, electrocardiograms (EKG), and MRI. EEG measures the electromagnetic fields of the brain. EKG measures the electromagnetic fields of the heart. MRI scans measure magnetic resonance in any area of the body that is examined. As fields of current and magnetism flow through our bodies, we experience this flow; that is, we experience somatic sensations arising within. When you experience a throbbing, an itch, a tingling, a pain, a contraction, or sense of expansion, or any other somatic sensation in your body, you are sensing electrochemical shifts that are occurring within your cells.

Most cells in the body generate an electrical field of roughly 70 mV, or .07 V of electricity. AA batteries generate 1.5 volts, and a typical wall socket is 115 volts. We also measure electromagnetic fields in Hz, representing the frequency of the cycles per second of these waves of energy. Your brain and heart generate an electromagnetic field resonating at frequencies of about 1-60 Hz. The heart averages about 7.8 Hz, and the brain typically functions in the range of 10-30 Hz. The standard electric Smart Meter on your house emits a field of 900-2,500 Hz, and the electromagnetic field generated by a cell phone can exceed 8,000 Hz.

The earth itself has a magnetic field in the cavity between the upper ionosphere and the surface of the earth, with a resonance ranging from 0.01 to 300 Hz, with an average 7.83 Hz. Dr. W.O. Schumann of the University of Munich first identified this resonance in 1953.[68] An electrician familiar with Schumann's work, Lewis B. Hainsworth, was among the first of modern-day scientists to suggest that the electromagnetic frequencies in the earth-ionosphere cavity play a governing role in the evolution of human and mammalian brainwave patterns, in DNA formation and physical and mental health in humans. Commenting on the similarity of brainwave activity and its relationship to the earth-ionospheric cavity resonance, Hainsworth said,

> *As human beings we have extraordinary potentials we have hardly begun to study, much less understand. Creative gifts, intuitions and talents that are unpredictable or emergent may become stabilized in generations to come. Hopefully, we can learn to understand both our emergence from an essentially electromagnetic environment and facilitate our potential for healing, growth and non-local communication.*[69]

Not only do chemicals activate the cellular mechanisms of our nerve cells and other tissues, but also the mere presence of an electromagnetic field can activate our bodies' cellular mechanisms. Even our genes function via electromagnetic mechanisms, transmitting electromagnetic or vibrational information to other cells, giving them functional directions.[70] Like the energy producing properties of an LED watch or light, our genes are liquid crystals, with specific vibrational properties that are the keys to our intrinsic functional, behavioral, and physical nature. These vibrational, electrophysiological experiences are the foundation of our senses, sum and substance of the experience of our being. By using meditation to attune ourselves with a sense of the world around us, we feel more harmonized, balanced, and in the flow.

CHAPTER 13

The Heart: Self-Awareness, Self-Control, and Entrainment

The electromagnetic energy generated by the heart is an untapped resource within the human system awaiting further exploration and application. Acting as a synchronizing force within the body, a key carrier of emotional information, and an apparent mediator of a type of subtle electromagnetic communication between people, the cardiac bioelectromagnetic field may have much to teach us about the inner dynamics of health and disease as well as our interactions with others.[71]

-Rollin McCraty
Institute of HeartMath (2003)

THE FEELING OF LOVE HAS a sensation. One night when my son Jon was about seven years old, I had kissed him and said goodnight and was walking out of his bedroom door when he murmured, "I love you Mommy." Being the sort of mother that I am, I turned in the doorway and gently asked, "What does that feel like?" After a long pause, he replied as he dozed off to sleep, "It feels like my heart is getting bigger." My own heart spilled over with the sensation of expansive love, and I smiled and said, "I love you too, Jon."

Out of the mouths of babes, love is the sensation of the heart growing bigger. There is a reason that we refer to the heart as the location of our experience of the emotion of love when we say things like, "I love you with all of my heart", "He broke my heart," or "My heart just wasn't in it." The yogic practice of i-Rest Yoga Nidra meditation, made popular by Dr. Richard Miller, makes use of the concept of *Heartfelt Desire* by connecting us with both our brains (thoughts) and our hearts (feelings) simultaneously. By being conscious of the thoughts or other activities that trigger the sensation of expansion in our hearts, we can come to know our heartfelt desire for determining direction in our life. We could also say that in yoga nidra meditation practice, we set the intention to open our hearts and let the heart's energy, or quite literally electromagnetic field, flow through the brain, as we become conscious of the thoughts thus generated. Through this exercise, we can also cultivate the practice of moving, finding direction in life, from both our heart and our head in partnership. We are truly in the flow when we are guided by both the heart and the head working together in unison.

The heart generates the most powerful electromagnetic field of all of the organs of the body. The electromagnetic field of the heart is even more powerful than the output of the brain. According to the HeartMath Institute, the amplitude of the heart's electrical field is sixty times greater than that of the brain's electrical field, while the magnetic field of the heart is five thousand times greater than that of the brain. The heart's magnetic field is so powerful that it is detectable by machine up to ten feet away from the human body.[72]

Heart coherence significantly increases during meditation. By activating our hearts through meditation, we emit a powerful electromagnetic field, one that permeates the space around us and creates a detectable sphere of magnetism throughout our bodies and into the space around us. Furthermore, coherence of the heart influences coherence of the brain, so that the resonant frequencies of these two organs become synchronized.[73] The nagging chatter of the critical mind ceases, and we feel a sense of knowing our own mind and heart, a sense of purpose and direction.

Research shows that humans are also sensitive to the electromagnetic field that emanates from other people around us.[74] Evidence for this effect comes from many sources. One area of medical use of this effect is the clinical use of entrainment to terminate arrhythmia, particularly atrial flutter. Exposing the heart with atrial flutter to a regulated electromagnetic field causes the heart muscle cells to become synchronized to this regulated electromagnetic field, thus slowing and making the heart's activity rhythmic.[75]

Just as the heart is sensitive to a mechanically generated electromagnetic field, one's heart is also sensitive to the electromagnetic field generated by other people's hearts. People in proximity with each other have been shown to *entrain*, as the electromagnetic fields of their brains and hearts become synchronized with each other. Entrainment is defined as the rhythmic synchronization of two or more beats, or the synchronization and control of cardiac rhythm by an external stimulus. This external stimulus may be mechanical or human. As we emit these detectable electromagnetic fields from our hearts into the space around us, our electromagnetic field is capable of influencing the function of other's hearts. Studies have shown that even in large groups of people, though measures of individual heart EMFs show multiple individual different EMFs at the outset, over time, one single EMF develops out of the group. All hearts begin to beat as one; that is, their electromagnetic fields become synchronized and appear to be the same.

Entrainment of the energy fields of our hearts and brains with those of other people can happen whether we are conscious of it or not. Like women in a college dorm who begin to share a monthly cycle, they don't get together and plan to start their periods at a certain time. It just happens. Similarly, people don't talk much about entraining their vibrational energy with each other—or do they? We do say things like, "She has a good vibe," or "I didn't like his energy." We speak of someone have a "calming" or "soothing" presence. As you learn to hold the field of awareness, to open your heart field conscious of the bioelectromechanics of entrain-ment, rather than entraining with anyone whom you encounter, you can hold your own field. You can maintain your own energetic state in the presence of others. You call the shots. You are empowered to choose to stay as you are, mindfully present and compassionate, and let others en-train with you.

While the concepts of entrainment are exciting in and of themselves, the real treasure in recognizing the energetic power of the heart is the potential to learn to consciously affect the EMFs that we generate and emit. I have found in my meditation classes that about half of all people are conscious of the pulsing of their own heartbeat. However, with practice, everyone can learn to become aware of their own heartbeat. And further-more, with continued meditation practice, as you cultivate the capacity for self-awareness, you will discover therein the capacity for self-regulation. You can learn to regulate your heart, becoming conscious of contracting your heart and opening it at will.

Empathy is the ability to open your heart and to let it entrain with another. When you empathize, you literally allow yourself to begin to have the experience of another person by letting your energy entrain with theirs. The energy fields of your heart and brain synchronize with theirs. Without consciousness of this empathic process, you can get lost in the pain and agony of others and in the highs and lows of all whom you en-counter. In the practice of "feeling for someone else," you can become incapacitated with their pain, which has now become yours. Empathy is a useful tool for understanding another person's emotional state, but it can render you dysfunctional and suffering.

Alternatively, compassion is the ability to open your heart and keep it open, even in the presence of the suffering of others. You can use empathy to sense another person's state to better understand it, but then return to your own energetic state. In this way you can remain functional and open-hearted. Like reaching out to touch a pot to see if it is hot or not, once you have touched it, you do not need to leave your hand there and possibly even burn your fingers. You have the knowledge of its state of being. You know that the pot is hot and you can handle it accordingly.

When you use empathy to explore and understand another person's feelings, you do not need to stay embroiled in their energetic state. Rather, in awareness, you can return to your own state of being. In the therapeutic process, use empathy to understand a subject's experience. Then consciously let it go and return to a compassionate state to avoid being dragged through the multiple and sometimes painful experiential shifts of the healing process. Also by consciously maintaining your own energetic state of compassion, you offer your client a healing presence through the opportunity to entrain with you in a more stable and healthy state of being.

The Sixth Sense: Sensing with the Heart

Heart coherence can be a cardiac marker for the meditative state and also may be a general marker for the meditative state since heart coherence is strongly correlated with EEG alpha activities. It is expected that increasing heart coherence and the accompanying EEG alpha activations, heart brain synchronicity, would help recover physiological synchrony following a period of homeostatic depletion.[76]

> -Dae-Keun Kim, Kyung-Mi Lee, Jongwha Kim, Min-Choel Whang and Seung Wan Kang.
> *Frontiers in Human Neuroscience* (1997)

Many forms of meditation have recognized the significance of "heart opening" exercises. Buddhist meditations include practices focused on opening the heart and cultivating compassion. Yoga nidra has exercises focused on recognizing sensations arising from the heart. Kundalini yoga uses physical postures, chanting, and breathing exercises to practice open-ing the heart chakra to move kundalini, or natural energy in the body, and "awaken."

There are so many mindfulness and related yoga practices focused on opening the heart that it made me wonder, why are we able to close our hearts in the first place. What adaptive mechanism should let us draw in the electromagnetic field that radiates from our hearts, and then make us struggle to reverse the process and once again allow our hearts to open and radiate?

One of the primary reasons that one might minimize the heart's de-tectable presence is fear. If love is the actual sensation of the heart open-ing, fear is the sensation of the heart squeezing tight. As we sense these emotions move through us or into us, we literally are expanding and con-tracting the electromagnetic field that emanates from the heart. Consider how the heart's energetic field is detectable at a distance and how it can influence the energy field of other living beings. If humans can learn to be conscious of this energetic sense, then certainly animals whose lives may depend upon it may also be aware of this sense and use it to detect the pres-ence of other animals. It makes sense that in a predator-prey relationship, other animals may live in more conscious awareness of the sensation of the presence of each other. We humans speak of this as a sixth sense—an awareness of the presence of other, even in the absence of other sensation such as vision or hearing. From the medical literature, we know this sen-sory capacity of our hearts to be true. Human hearts can sense and entrain with both mechanically generated EMFs and with EMFs that emanate from other living organisms.[77] If other animals are conscious of this sensa-tion, recognizing when they sense the presence of another living being's heart field, then they could use this sense for survival. So it makes sense in a predator-prey relationship, or other circumstances in which one's life is at stake, that a reflexive reaction to sensing imminent danger would be to draw in the heart's energetic field. Contracting the heart field is a way of hiding, so that one cannot be detected by another.

If the cat can sense the mouse by sensing the mouse's heart field, it would behoove the mouse to be able to sense the cat's heart field as well. And when the mouse senses the cat, the mouse would do well to draw in its energy field, thus hiding itself from the cat. This is an innate response to fear. Humans have this same instinctive and reflexive nature to draw in the heart's energetic radiance. We've simply lost conscious awareness of what we are doing.

By drawing in or closing the heart, one is hiding from another sensate being, as if to say, "I do not exist." People suffering from PTSD and depression often report that they feel like they don't exist. It has been suggested that self-injurious behavior such as cutting oneself is committed in an attempt to at least feel something. The problem is in the heart. Fear has contracted the heart and deadened the ability to feel. When we are safe, we can sooth and again open the heart. We can again begin to feel. Meditation practices focused on somatic sensing can be used to gradually reintroduce the realm of sensate experiences. It may be helpful to do this work in the company of an experienced meditation teacher who knows how to use the breath to maintain a sense of safety and groundedness.

Through the practice of heart-focused or compassion-focused meditations, conscious awareness of the heart's electrical and magnetic dimensions can be cultivated. Correspondingly, researchers have found that compassion-based or heart-focused meditation practices result in changes in the areas of the brain that regulate the heart.[78] We see growth in both the grey matter and white matter of the brain. Once again, by cultivating self-consciousness, we improve our capacity for self-regulation, becoming capable of coordinating the activity of our hearts.

The idea of being conscious of the sensations of the heart, and the emotional interpretation of these senses, is not that far removed from the way we intuitively talk about these phenomena. We often use expressions referring to some sensate quality of the heart. These expressions may be more than just a poetic metaphor; they appear to represent the real capacity of our heart sense. For example, we use many of these familiar expressions to describe the heart:

An "open heart" is one that is radiant and receptive and capable of being present for others. Its energetic field is expansive.

A "closed heart" is one that has suffered and is not trusting, or is fearful. Its energetic field has been drawn in tight.

A "cold heart" is also closed and has no apparent sense of connection, empathy, or compassion with others.

A "hardened heart" is one that does not readily respond to either fear or love. Its energetic field is present but held close and tight.

A "faint heart" is one that lacks stamina, is easily swayed, and energetically depleted.

A "lonely heart" is one that has not had connection with others in too long a period of time and has begun to close and perhaps ache for the sense of connection with another heart. It is also energetically withdrawn.

A "broken heart" is one that was energetically open and connected, but has lost the connection upon which it thrived. It can readily rebound in connection with another, but should be given time to heal/open on its own.

An "angry heart" is a heart that has managed to open, but struggles to stay that way.

"Courage" from the Latin word "cor" for heart, implies the ability to keep the heart open, even in the face of danger.

Of all of the risk factors predictive of heart disease, including biological risk factors such as high cholesterol or elevated inflammatory markers such as C - reactive protein or interleukin-6, the most predictive risk factors are these emotional factors stemming from the heart. More so than the physical correlates of heart disease, emotional trauma places people at significant risk for cardiovascular heart disease and death independent of established biological risk factors. Many studies have identified suppressed anger (a heart working hard but unable to open) as the most potent risk factor for heart attack.[79] [80]

The ability of the heart to contract or to expand its energetic field corresponds with the contractile nature of the cardiovascular system. When an artery or vein is touched, it quickly contracts, almost disappearing. Once left alone, it will only gradually reopen and begin to flow to its full capacity. An artery or vein that is repeatedly prodded or poked will eventually begin to stay in the more contracted state. The same is true of the heart itself. Repeated exposure to threatening stimuli may cause a sustained contraction of both the muscle and nerve fibers of the cardiovascular system, as well as the energetic field that these fibers emit. In situations of repeated threat or trauma, or even a single major traumatic incident, the entire cardiovascular system in conjunction with its networks with the brain may learn to withdraw and contract. A heart that fears to reopen and expand fully back into its energetic space is in the condition we identify as post-traumatic stress. Trauma, associated with fear, causes the heart to draw in its energy field. The Thalamic Gates close and somatic consciousness is minimized. A heart that has learned to contract in the presence of what it considers a threatening stimulus in its environment is incapacitated. It can no longer fully perform its functions. Whether these functions involve facilitating the circulatory system, or sensing the living world around us, a closed heart is not open to guide us—to help us to feel our way through life.

By deconditioning or habituating this cardio-vascular hypersensitivity and corresponding energetic withdrawal, we can learn to relieve symptoms of trauma and post-traumatic stress. This deconditioning of cardiovascular hypersensitivity is achieved by practicing heart opening meditation exercises.

Dog and other animal therapies are effectively used for the treatment of veterans and other people who have suffered severe trauma and PTSD. Though researchers have limited their hypothesis to biochemical phero-mones to explain why the company of dogs works to sooth symptoms of emotional trauma, it is equally possible that it has something to do with entrainment to the energy field of a dog's heart. Dogs have great big heart energy fields, and few natural predators from which they must hide. They have very few natural reasons to subdue the EMF that extends from their hearts. They are also quite social animals, living in packs, and perhaps using their heart fields to stay connected with and to sense each other. With powerful hearts, dogs are very perceptive of fear and have also been employed to detect would-be villains. I think that dogs are able to sense fear and villainous intentions because they use their heart to sense the in-stability of a villain's heart field. Dogs can also apparently use their heart fields to open ours, and to heal the wounds of trauma and fear.

Humans can also learn to regulate their heart fields through medita-tion. Just as we can focus on the ebb and flow rhythm of the breath, we can focus on the pulsing rhythms of the heart. The breath also influences the waves of cardiac depolarization and the rhythm of the heart's pulse.[81] Eventually you can learn to sense the opening of the heart and the expan-sive sensation of the heart's energy field growing within. Compassion-based meditation has the practitioner focus on memories of the sensation of love. Once you learn to associate the sensation that arises within your heart when you feel the passion of love from the cognitive memories of love, you will discover the capacity to elicit this sensation at will. You will not need to use memories to activate the opening of your heart. Simply the intention to feel the radiance of your own heart field will change the electromagnetic state of your heart and the energy that permeates from your heart, through you, and around you.

As the heart's energy field expands and becomes more present in your consciousness, you can become aware of the sensation of the connection of heart and mind, the synchronization of the energy fields of the brain and the heart. You will have a sense of peacefulness with yourself.

The mind can influence the heart, or the heart can guide the mind. Given the greater amplitude and power of the heart, it can often rule. Given the greater discretion and the subtle nuances of the energy fields of the brain, it is relevant to attend to the brain as well.

We have become a culture guided primarily by our brains. In forgetting to connect with our hearts and losing sensate awareness of the physical body, which is the source of our emotions and feelings, we have become reliant on the logic of the brain. We end up longing for the heart's sense of guidance that allows us to know direction and purpose in life. That feeling of knowing your course of action, your heart-felt desires, comes from the connection between heart and brain.

By opening your heart and your mind and using both to sense and be guided by the flow of the energy fields of the earth and indeed the universe around you, in the peacefulness of that momentum, you will discover a sense of direction and purpose.

THE FELT-SENSE OF CONNECTION

One love, one heart... Let's get together and feel all right.[82]

-Bob Marley

There are many ways in which a sense of connection has proven to enhance well-being, quality of life and longevity. It is a long established fact that married couples outlive their single peers, experience fewer complaints and conditions, and report a better quality of life as they age. Similarly, support groups that provide a sense of community have proven effective in increasing rates of survival and longevity. Also, Dan Buettner's study of longevity in his seminal work about "Blue Zones", recognized the role of social connection in prolonging people's lives and enhancing quality of life, even as important if not more so than eating healthy foods and getting enough exercise and sleep.[83] Buettner also identified the powerful role of the sense of spiritual connection in increasing longevity, as have many other researchers. Other studies have shown that strong bonds and relationships with our pets can even have life enhancing effects, such as the studies I discussed earlier involving veterans suffering from PTSD who recovered by developing emotional bonds with dogs.

Studies using fMRI have found that the experience of social connection with other people is associated with activity in the brain regions of the temporal and parietal lobes.[84] Separate f-MRI studies have found that during prayer, the sense of spiritual connection similarly activated the temporal and parietal lobes and related brain regions.[85] These studies suggest similar brain regions regulate senses of human and spiritual connection. In both of these studies the common element activating these same brain regions was time spent opening to the felt-sense of connection. During this time, the mind and heart, indeed the entire body allows the experience of a sense of flow between self and other, an experience in which separateness dissolves. Feelings of isolation or loneliness are transformed by releasing the barriers we have held to connection with other.

I am sure that as with any practice affecting the brain, brain regions associated with the experience of connection can grow as we spend time in curious awareness of the sense of connection. Whether you open to experiencing this connection with a loved-one or pet, your community, and or a spiritual sense of connection, awareness of this felt-sense of connection grows out of mindful introspection. Through mindfulness practices we can gradually access the fullness of the felt-sense of connection by opening our minds, our hearts, indeed our entire being, in curious aware-ness of these experiences. Not only will the associated regions of the brain become active and begin to grow, but also as you experience this relational sense of flow, you may well experience a greater sense of well-being and vitality.

Buettner associated this sense of connection and relationship with other, with the sense of purpose, which he also identified as a common in-gredient in all centenarian populations. The sense of connectedness avail-able during mindful introspection may well be the driving force behind cultivating a sense of purpose. And it seems from Buettner's research that this relational experience, that drives our sense of purpose, also provides the momentum for longevity, good life and well-being.

CHAPTER 14

Consciousness and Intention

WE MAY GO THROUGH LIFE not conscious of the momentum of our lives or the intentions that we have set for ourselves. We may be aiming toward some distant point in our life, without awareness that our actions are carrying us toward this intention. Have you ever headed off in a car to a new destination and found yourself headed toward a more familiar place? We become familiar with a certain path, a way of living, or a way of being and then find ourselves along the way headed down this familiar path. We establish a certain momentum early in life and then we let this momentum carry us down this preset path. The path may involve whom we expect to become, how we expect to live, the image we portray of the type of person we are, what we expect to make of our lives, or even when we expect to marry, have children, retire, or to die.

At any point in our lives we can become conscious of where we are along our journey. As in the example of driving, we can stop. We can pause to take notice of where we are and take in the experience of the moment, the momentum. Like pulling into an overlook, stepping out of the car and enjoying the view, we can pause from the commotion of life, look up, and take in the full physical experience of wherever we are in the momentum of life. In this moment of conscious awareness, we can reset our intentions. We can reconsider the direction of our life. In this moment of mindfulness, we can change our minds and our lives.

Give yourself time to sit long enough to let go of resistance that presents itself. Give yourself the chance to let the mind and the heart open and connect. An open mind is curious and aware of the sense of the momentum of life. Feel the flow of your breath, the pulse of your heart, and the other rhythms of the universe that permeate your being and make up the symphony of your life. Let go of any effort to focus. Open the Thalamic Gates and enter into the realm of deeper consciousness, feeling the sensate experience of your entire being. Become aware of the broad landscape of experience. Then let your awareness focus one more place. Direct your awareness to observe itself. Become aware of your own awareness. Wherein resides the witness of your experience? Open your consciousness to the sensate qualities of consciousness. Become consciousness itself.

When you have finished your meditation practice, take note of how you feel when you are done. Continue to check in on yourself throughout the day. Mindfulness is not just an occasional practice. It is a way of being. You become mindful. Just as exercise makes you strong, and you become strong, mindfulness practices make you mindful. You will notice your consciousness present as you go through your day. When you greet other people, check in. Notice what it is like to experience their presence. When you eat your meals, notice the sensation of nourishment. When you go to bed, breathe into that feeling of surrender and letting go of conscious awareness. And, as you awaken again in the morning, greet the consciousness as it stirs you from your slumber. Notice what it is like to breathe. Notice what it is like to be! Meditation is a practice. Being mindful is a state of being in the flow. Practicing mindfulness meditation is a way of being in the flow and using mindfulness to find your heart's passion and fulfill your life's purpose!

Disclaimer

THE INFORMATION CONTAINED IN THIS book is for educational purposes only. The use of the information in this book is at the user's own risk. It is not intended to diagnose, prescribe, or treat any medical condition, illness, or injury. The author, publishers, and distributors of this book shall have no liability or responsibility to any person or entity with respect to any and all alleged damage, loss, or injury caused or allegedly caused directly or indirectly by the information contained in this book. Nothing contained in this book is intended as a substitute for medical advice. All readers are encouraged to obtain medical advice from a qualified medical professional.

The Mindfulness Center

**Founders Deborah Norris, Ph.D.,
Jacqueline Norris, and Jessie Taylor**

THE MINDFULNESS CENTER IS A 501(c)3 non-profit organization that promotes health and self-healing, for individuals and the community, through evidence-based charitable, educational and research programs in mind-body practices. The mission of The Mindfulness Center is to facilitate the evolution of the standard of health care from one of managing disease to one of fostering health, and to be a model for a new health care paradigm. The Mindfulness Center fulfills this mission by bringing mindfulness to all dimensions of life, and empowering people to use evidence-based, best practices of self-care, thereby addressing health care disparities by making health care accessible to all. The Mindfulness Center is based in Bethesda, Maryland.

Visit www.TheMindfulnessCenter.org for more information.

Other Multi-Media Programs by Deborah Norris, Ph.D. available at www.TheMindfulnessCenter.org

The Power of Mindfulness: **Online Meditation Programs**
Online Introduction to Meditation. An online, community-based program for the beginning meditation student, and those who wish to deepen their meditation practice, and join a community of fellow meditators in exploring the depths of the practice and the experiential outcomes of meditation.
Online Meditation Teacher Training. A 160-hour, online, community-based, immersive program preparing experienced meditators to become qualified, certified meditation teachers.

Every Child Thrives: **Mindfulness Programs for Children**
Guided Meditation for Children's Health. A five-minute audio, guided meditation used in children's healthcare settings to relieve stress, anxiety and pain associated with medical procedures.
Mindfulness Meditation for Families with Children with Attention Deficit Hyperactivity Disorder. An evidence-based program providing guided meditation practices and helpful information for families with children with ADHD and other learning disabilities. Mindfulness meditation has proven to relieve symptoms associated with the diagnosis of ADHD.

Part 1: Finding the Flow

4. Health Effects of Meditation

1. Stinley, Nora E. Norris, D. Hinds, P. (2014). Non-pharmacological management of acute pain symptoms in pediatric patients. *Annals of Society of Behavioral Medicine.*

2. Kabat-Zinn, J., Wheeler, E., Light, T., Skillings, A., Scharf, M.J., Cropley, T.G., Hosmer, D., Bernhard, J.D. (1998). Influence of a mindfulness meditation-based stress reduction intervention on rates of skin clearing in patients with moderate to severe psoriasis undergoing phototherapy (UVB) and photochemotherapy (PUVA). *Psychosomatic Medicine, 60*(5), 625-632.

3. Loucks, E.B. Schuman-Olivier, Z., Britton, W.B., Fresco, D.M., Desbordes, G., Brewer, J.A., Fulwiler, C. (2015). Mindfulness and Cardiovascular Disease Risk: State of the Evidence, Plausible Mechanisms, and Theoretical Framework. Current Cardiology Reports, 17, 112.

4. Hartmann, M., Kopf, S., Kircher, C., Faude-Lang, V., Zdenka, D., Augstein, F., Friederich, H.C., Kieser, M., Bierhaus, A., Humpert, P.M., Herzog, W., Nawroth, P.P. (2012). Sustained effects of a mindfulness based stress-reduction intervention in type 2 diabetic patients: design and first results of a randomized controlled trial (the Heidelberger Diabetes and Stress-study). *Diabetes Care, 35*(5), 945-947.

5. Caria, A.S. (2012). Real–Time fMRI: A Tool for Local Brain Regulation. *Neuroscientist, 18,* 487–501.

6. Segal, Z.V., Bieling, P., Young, T., MacQueen, G., Cooke, R., Martin, L., Bloch, R., Levitan, R.D. (2010). Antidepressant monotherapy versus sequential pharmacotherapy and mindfulness–based cognitive therapy, or placebo, for relapse prophylaxis in recurrent depression. *Archives of General Psychiatry, 67*(12), 1256-1264.

7. Serafeim, A., Grafton, G., Chamba, A., Gregory, C.D., Blakely, R.D., Bowery, N.G., Barnes, N.M., Gordon, J. (2002). 5–Hydroxytryptamine drives apoptosis in biopsylike Burkitt lymphoma cells: reversal by selective serotonin reuptake inhibitors. *Blood, 99*(7), 2545-25⊠53.

8. Serafeim, A., Holder, M.J., Grafton, G., Chamba, A., Drayson, M.T., Luong, Q.T., Bunce, C.M., Gregory, C.D., Barnes, N.M., Gordon, J. (2003). Selective serotonin reuptake inhibitors directly signal for apoptosis in biopsy–like Burkitt lymphoma cells. *Blood, 101*(8), 3212-3219.

9. Beena, R.K. (2013). Yogic practice and diabetes mellitus in geriatric patients. *International Journal of Yoga, 6* (1), 47–54.

10. Murdock, Kyle W., Angie S. Leroy, Tamara E. Lacourt, Danny C. Duke, Cobi J. Heijnen, and Christopher P. Fagundes. "Executive Functioning and Diabetes: The Role of Anxious Arousal and Inflammation." *Psychoneuroendocrinology* 71 (2016): 102-09. Web.

11. Zhang Y, Li N, Sun J, Su Q. Effects of combined traditional Chinese exercises on blood pressure and arterial function of adult female hypertensive patients. *Res Sports Med.* 2013;21(1):98-109.

12. Tang, Y., Ma, Y., Wang, J., Fan, Y., Feng, S., Lu, Q.... Posner, M. I. (2007). Short-term meditationtraining improves attention and self-regulation. *Proceedings of the National Academy of Sciences,* 104(43), 17152-17156.

13. Young, S. (2011, March). Biologic effects of mindfulness meditation: Growing insights into neurobiologic aspects of the prevention of depression. *Journal of Psychiatry & Psychiatry & Neuroscience*, 36(2), 75-77.

14. Faber, P. L., Lehmann, D., Gianotti, L. R., Milz, P., Pascual-Marqui, R. D., Held, M., & Kochi, K. (2014). Zazen meditation and no-task resting EEG compared with LORETA intracortical source localization. *Cognitive Processing, 16*(1), 87-96.

15. Tomljenovic, H., Begic, D., & Mastrovik, Z. (2016, March). Changes in trait brainwave power and coherence, state and trait anxiety after three-month transcendental meditation (TM) practice. *Psychiatria Danubina, 28*(1), 63-72.

16. Cahn, B. R., Delorme, A., & Polich, J. (2012). Event-related delta, theta, alpha and gamma correlates to auditory oddball processing during Vipassana meditation. *Social Cognitive and Affective Neuroscience, 8*(1), 100-111.

17. Mcewen, B. S. (2016). In pursuit of resilience: Stress, epigenetics, and brain plasticity. *Annals of the New York Academy of Sciences.*

18. Creswell, J. D., Irwin, M. R., Burklund, L. J., Lieberman, M. D., Arevalo, J. M., Ma, J., . . . Cole, S. W. (2012). Mindfulness-Based Stress Reduction training reduces loneliness and pro-inflammatory gene expression in older adults: A small randomized controlled trial. *Brain, Behavior, and Immunity, 26*(7), 1095-1101.

19. Sturtevant, A. H. (1913). The linear arrangement of six sex-linked factors in Drosophila, as shown by their mode of association. *Journal of Experimental Zoology*, 14: 43-59.

20. Sanger, F.; Nicklen, S.; Coulson, A.R. (1977), "DNA sequencing with chain-terminating inhibitors," *Proceedings of the National Academy of Sciences USA* 74 (12): 5463–5467.

21. International Human Genome Sequencing Consortium. (2001). *Nature, 409,* 860-921.

22. Lavretsky, H., Epel, E.S., Siddarth, P., Nazarian, N., Cyr, N.S., Khalsa, D.S., Lin, J., Blackburn, E., Irwin, M.R. (2013). A pilot study of yogic meditation for family dementia caregivers with depressive symptoms: effects on mental health, cognition, and telomerase activity. *International Journal of Geriatric Psychiatry, 28*(1), 57–65.

23. Jacobs, T. L., Epel, E. S., Lin, J., Blackburn, E. H., Wolkowitz, O. M., Bridwell, D. A., . . Saron, C. D. (2011, June). Intensive meditation training, immune cell telomerase activity, and psychological mediators. *Psychoneuroendocrinology, 36*(5), 664-681.

24. ibid

25. ibid

26. Omura, Y., Shimotsura, Y., Ooki, M., Noguchi, T. (1998). Estimation of the amount of telomere molecules in different human age groups and the telomere increasing effect of acupuncture and shiatsu on St.36, using synthesized basic units of the human telomere molecules as reference control substances for the bi-digital O-ring test resonance phenomenon. *Acupuncture & Electro-therapeutics Research, 23*(3–4), 185–206.

27. Carlson, L. E., Beattie, T. L., Giese-Davis, J., Faris, P., Tamagawa, R., Fick, L. J. ... Speca, M. (2015). Mindfulness-based cancer recovery and supportive-expressive therapy maintain telomere length relative to controls in distressed breast cancer survivors. *Cancer,* 121(3), 476-484.

28. Carlson, L. E., Beattie, T. L., Giese-Davis, J., Faris, P., Tamagawa, R., Fick, L. J. ... Speca, M. (2015). Mindfulness-based cancer recovery and supportive-expressive therapy maintain telomere length relative to controls in distressed breast cancer survivors. *Cancer*, 121(3), 476-484.

29. Witek-Janusek, L. Albuquerque, K., Chroniak, K. R., Chroniak, C., Durazo-Arvizu, R., & Mathews, H. L. (2008). Effect of mindfulness based stress reduction on immune function, quality of life and coping in women newly diagnosed with early stage breast cancer. *Brain, Behavior, and Immunity*, 22(6), 969-981.

30. Carlson, L. E., Beattie, T. L., Giese-Davis, J., Faris, P., Tamagawa, R., Fick, L. J. ... Speca, M. (2015). Mindfulness-based cancer recovery and supportive-expressive therapy maintain telomere length relative to controls in distressed breast cancer survivors. *Cancer*, 121(3), 476-484.

Part 2: Thalamic Gating: Expanding Consciousness with the Breath

5. Body Awareness

31. Wolpe, J. (1958). *Psychotherapy by reciprocal inhibition*. Stanford, CA: Stanford University Press, 53-62.

32. Holzel, B.K., Lazar, S.W., Gard, T., Schuman-Oliver, Z., Vago, D.R., and Ott, U. (2011). How does mindfulness meditation work? Proposing mechanisms of action from a conceptual and neural perspective. *Perspective on Psychological Science*, 6(6), 537-559.

33. Alexander, GM, Kurukulasuriya, N.C., Mu, J., Godwin, D.W. (2006). Cortical feedback to the thalamus is selectively enhanced by nitric oxide. *Neuroscience, 142(1)*, 223-234.

34. Melzack, R., & Wall, P. D. (1965). Pain Mechanisms: A New Theory. *Science, 150*(3699), 971-979.

35. Holzel, B.K., Lazar, S.W., Gard, T., Schuman-Oliver, Z., Vago, D.R., and Ott, U. (2011). How does mindfulness meditation work? Proposing mechanisms of action from a conceptual and neural perspective. *Perspective on Psychological Science, 6*(6), 537-559.

36. Nassif, T. H., Norris, D. O., Sandbrink, F., Chapman, J. C., Soltes, K. L., Reinhard, M. J., & Blackman, M. (2015, November 17). Mindfulness meditation and chronic pain management in Iraq and Afghanistan veterans with traumatic brain injury: A pilot study. *Military Behavioral Health, 4*(1).

6. Mindfulness: The Foundation for Behavioral Change

37. Scholkmann, F., Fels, D., and Cifra, M. (2013) Cell-to-Cell Communication: Current Views and Future Perspectives. *Cell Tissue Research*, 352(1), 1-3.

38. Buzsaki, G. Llinas,R.Singer, W., Berthoz, A.,Christen, Y. (2012). *Temporal Coding in the Brain*. Springer Science & Business Media.

39. Rush, C. (2013). Mindfulness mediates neuroticism as a predictor of self-control and impulsivity: Potential implications for behavioral regulation, (Unpublished masters dissertation). American University, Washington, D.C.

40. Sakurai, T. (2007). The neural circuit of orexin(hypocretin): maintaining sleep and wakefulness. *Nature Reviews Neuroscience*, 8, 171-181.

41. Williams, R. H., Jensen, L.T., Verkhratsky, A., Fugger, L., Burdakov, D. (2007). Control of Hypothalamic orexin neurons by acid and CO2. Proceedings of the National Academy of Science. 104(25)10685-90.

42. Williams, R.H., Burdakov, D. (2008). Hypothalamic orexins/hypocretins as regulators of breathing. Expert Reviews in Molecular Medicine.

43. Sakuri, T. (2007) The neural circuit of orexin (hypocretin): maintaining sleep and wakefulness. Nat Rev Neuroscience, 8, 171-181.

44. Carlson, L.E. (2012, November). Mindfulness-Based Interventions for Physical Conditions: A Narrative Review Evaluating Levels of Evidence. *ISRN Psychiatry.*

45. Balaji, P.A., Varne, S.R., Ali, S.S. (2012). Physiological Effects of Yogic Practices and Transcendental Meditation in Health and Disease. *North American Journal of Medical Science*, 4 (10), 4420448.

7. Ooh, Las Vagus Nerve! How to Control Your Behavior

46. Montiel-Castro, A.J., Gonzalez-Cervantes, R.M., Bravo-Ruiseco, G.B., Pacheco-Lopez, G. (2013) The microbiota-gut-brain axis: neurobehavioral correlates, health and sociality. *Frontiers of Integrative Neuroscience*, 7:70.

47. Forsythe, P., Bienenstock, J. Kunze, W.A. (2014). Vagal pathways for microbiome-brain-gut axis communication. *Advances in Experimental Medical Biology*, 817: 115-133.

48. Mayer, E. A., Knight, R., Mazmanian, S.K., Cryan, J.F., Tillisch, K. (2014). Gut Microbes and the brain: Paradigm shift in neuroscience. *Journal of Neuroscience*, 34(46): 15490-15496.

49. *Ibid.*

50. Wang, Y., Kasper, L.H. (2014). The Role of Microbiome in Central Nervous System Disorders. *Brain Behavior and Immunity*, 38:1-12.

51. Dinan, T.G., Cryan, J.F. (2015). The impact of gut microbiota on brain and behavior: Implications for psychiatry. *Current Opinion in Clinical Nutrition & Metabolic Care*, 18(6):552-8.

52. Tracey, K. J. (2002). The inflammatory reflex. *Nature*, 420(6917): 853-859.

53. Mosialou, I., Shikkel, S., Liu, J.M., Maurizi, A., Luo, N., et al. (2017). MC4R-dependent suppression of appetite by bone-derived lipocalin 2., *Nature*, 543(7645):385-390.

8. The Breath

54. Warburg, O., Wind, F. & Negelein, E. (1927). The metabolism of tumors in the body. *Journal of General Physiology*, 8(6):519-530.

55. *Ibid.*

9. The Senses

56. James W. (1884). What is an emotion? *Mind*, 9, 188–205.

10. The Mind: Dealing with Thoughts

57. Bender, S., Migdow, J. (2010). *Goddess to the Core: An Inspired Workout to Maximize Your Fitness, Beauty & Power*. Llewellyn Publications.

58. James W. (1884). What is an emotion? *Mind*, 9, 188–205.

59. Woese, C. R. (1987, June). Bacterial evolution. *Microbiological Reviews*, *51*(2), 221-271.

60. James W. (1884). What is an emotion? *Mind*, 9, 188–205.

Part 3: Heart Sensing

11. Momentum

61. Newton, I., Motte, A., Machin, J., & Motte, B. (1729). *The Mathematical Principles of Natural Philosophy*. London: Printed for Benjamin Motte.

12. Perspectives on Being: Creating Sensate Awareness

62. Guenon, R. (1942). *The Crisis of the Modern World*. London, Luzac and Company.

63. Craig, A.D. (2002). How do you feel? Interoception: the sense of the physiological condition of the body. *Nature Reviews in Neuroscience*, 3(8):655-66.

64. Craig, A.D. (2003). Interoception: the sense of the physiological condition of the body. *Current Opinion in Neurobiology*, 13:500-505.

65. Caria, A., Veit, R., Sitaram, R., Lotze, M., Weiskopf, N., Grodd, W., Birbaumer, N. (2007). Regulation of anterior insular cortex activity using real-time fMRI. *Neuroimage, 35*(3), 1238-1246.

66. James W. (1884). What is an emotion? *Mind*, 9, 188–205

67. Cherry, N.J. (2003). Human intelligence: the brain, an electromagnetic system synchronized by the Schumann Resonance. *Medical Hypotheses*, 60(6):843-4.

68. Schumann, W.O. (1952). Ueber die strahlungslosen Eigenschwingungen einer leitenden Kugel, die von einer Luftschicht und einer Ionosphaerenhuelle umgeben ist, Z.Naturforsch. 7a, 149.

69. Hainsworth, L.B. (1983). The effect of geophysical phenomena on human health. *Speculations in Science and Technology*, 6(5), 439-444.

70. Daza, A., Wagemakers, A., Shanmuganathan R., Sanjuan, M.A.F. (2013). Vibrational resonance in a time-delayed genetic toggle switch. *Communications in Nonlinear Science and Numerical Simulation, 18*(2), 411-416.

13. THE HEART: SELF-AWARENESS, SELF-CONTROL, AND ENTRAINMENT

71. McCraty, R. (2003). *The Energetic Heart: Bioelectromagnetic Interactions Within and Between People*. Boulder Creek, CA: Institute of HeartMath.

72. *Ibid.*

73. Kim, D.K., Lee, K.M., Kim, J., Whang, M.C., Kang, S.W. (2013). Dynamic correlations between heart and brain rhythm during Autogenic meditation. *Frontiers in Human Neuroscience, 7*, 414.

74. McCraty, R. (2003). *The Energetic Heart: Bioelectromagnetic Interactions Within and Between People.* Boulder Creek, CA: Institute of HeartMath.

75. Waldo, A. L. (1997, March). Atrial Flutter: Entrainment characteristics. *Journal of Cardiovascular Electrophysiology, 8*(3), 337-352.

76. Kim, D.K., Lee, K.M., Kim, J., Whang, M.C., Kang, S.W. (2013). Dynamic correlations between heart and brain rhythm during Autogenic meditation. *Frontiers in Human Neuroscience, 7*, 414.

77. McCraty, R. (2003). *The Energetic Heart: Bioelectromagnetic Interactions Within and Between People.* Boulder Creek, CA: Institute of HeartMath.

78. Tang, Y.Y., Ma, Y., Fan, Y., Feng, H., Wang, J., Feng, S., Lu, Q., Hu, B., Lin, Y., Li, J., Zhang, Y., Wang, Y., Zhou, L., Fan, M. (2009). Central and autonomic nervous system interaction is altered by short-term meditation. *Proceedings of the National Academy of Sciences of the United States of America, 106*(22). 8865-8870.

79. Alexander, F.G. (1939). Emotional factors in essential hypertension: Presentation of a tentative hypothesis. *Psychosomatic Medicine, 1*, 175-179.

80. Diamond, E.L. (1982). The role of anger and hostility in essential hypertension and coronary heart disease. *Psychological Bulletin, 92*, 410-433.

81. Mimbs, J.W., deMello, V., Roberts, R. The effect of respiration on normal and abnormal Q waves. An electrocardiographic and vector-cardiographic analysis. *American Heart Journal, 94*(5), 579-584.

82. Bob Marley and Curtis Mayfield, One Love / People Get Ready. Exodus, 1977.

83. Buettner, D. (2008). The Blue Zone: Lessons for Living Longer from the People Who've Lived the Longest. *National Geographic Books.*

84. Lahnakoski JM, Glerean E, Salmi J, Jääskeläinen IP, Sams M, Hari R, Nummenmaa L. (2012). Naturalistic FMRI mapping reveals superior temporal sulcus as the hub for the distributed brain network for social perception. *Front Hum Neurosci.* 13(6):233.

85. Schjoedt, U., Stødkilde-Jørgensen, H., Geertz, A.W., Roepstorff, A. (2009). Highly religious participants recruit areas of social cognition in personal prayer. Soc Cogn Affect Neurosci, 4(2):199-207.